Transportation Economics

Transportation Economics

Herbert Mohring

Ballinger Publishing Company • **Cambridge, Mass.**
A Subsidiary of J. B. Lippincott Company

This book is printed on recycled paper.

International Standard Book Number: 0-88410-419-2

Library of Congress Catalog Card Number: 75-35999

Printed in the United States of America

Library of Congress Cataloging in Publication Data

Mohring, Herbert.
    Transportation economics.
    Includes bibliographical references.
    1. Transportation. I. Title.
HE151.M66   380.5   75-35999
ISBN 0-88410-419-2

To Mom, Dad, Popie, and the Tigers

Contents

List of Tables xi

List of Figures xiii

Acknowledgments xv

Chapter One
Introduction: Is Transportation Different? 1

Chapter Two
Competitive Equilibrium 5

Chapter Three
Congestion and the Optimization of
 Transportation Activities 15

Appendix to Chapter Three
The Relationships Among Congestion Tolls, Capacity Costs,
 and the Value of the Marginal Product of Capacity 23

Chapter Four
Differences in Travel Time Values and the
 Optimization of Transportation Facilities 25

Appendix to Chapter Four
The Role of the Value of Travel Time in the Optimization
 and Pricing of Transportation Services 37

Chapter Five
The Value of Travel Time   41

The Choice of Speed Market   44
The Choice of Location Market   46
The Route and Mode Choice Markets   47
Reconciling the Market Data   54

Chapter Six
The Peak Load and Related Cost
Allocation Problems   59

Mutton and Wool and the Back-Haul Problem:
  Cost Allocation with Fixed Proportions   60
The Peak Load Problem   62
Mutton and Wool Again: Euler's Theorem and
  Cost Allocation   67
The Highway Cost Allocation Problem and
  Alternative Technologies   70

Chapter Seven
The Shapes of Transportation Cost Schedules—
Delays, Congestion, and Random Demands   75

The Shape of a Railroad's Short Run Cost Schedule   76
Random Demands and Indivisibilities   80

Chapter Eight
Measuring the Benefits of Transportation
System Investment Projects   85

Measuring Individual Benefits   86
Aggregating Individual Benefit Measures   89
The Cancellation of Benefits and Costs in Aggregating
  Investment Effects   91
Aggregate Benefits When Marginal Cost Tolls Are Not Charged   98

Chapter Nine
Consumers' Surplus versus National Income
Change Benefit Measures   105

Chapter Ten
Transportation Improvements and Land Values   115

Chapter Eleven

The "Industrial Reorganization" Benefits of
   Transportation Improvements   127

Chapter Twelve

Economies and Diseconomies of Scale in
   Transportation Activities   135

The "Six-Tenths Rule"   137
Scale Economies (and Diseconomies) in the Geometry of
   Transportation Rights-of-Way   140
The "Square Root Principle" and Bus Line Costs   145
Massed Reserves Scale Economics and Airline Scheduling   157

References   165

Index   171

About the Author   175

List of Tables

3-1.   Average and Marginal Travel Time per Vehicle Mile on
       City Streets at Alternative Volume-Capacity Ratios   17
12-1. Marginal and Average Costs of Highway Capacity in
       Areas of Different Net Residential Densities   143
12-2. Optimum Service Levels, Fares, and Subsidies for Three-
       Mile Trips on Steady State Bus Routes   153
12-3. Costs for Three-Mile Trips on Optimized Steady State
       Bus Routes   154
12-4. Variations in Optimum Average Load Factors and Airline
       Costs per Coach Passenger with Market Sizes and Distances 163

List of Figures

2-1. Types of Short Run Cost Schedules   7
2-2. Short Run Equilibrium of a Competitive Business Firm   9
2-3. Short and Long Run Equilibrium of a Competitive Industry   11
3-1. Marginal and Average Costs of City Street Trips   19
6-1. Peak Load Equilibrium of Business Firm with Type I Costs   64
6-2. Peak Load Equilibrium of Business Firm with Type II Costs   65
6-3. Alternative Highway Short Run Cost Schedules for a Given
      Capital Outlay   73
8-1. Consumer's Surplus   88
8-2. Direct Benefits of Road Improvement with Marginal Cost
      Tolls   93
8-3. Direct and Indirect Effects of Road Improvement with
      Marginal Cost Tolls   96
8-4. Direct and Indirect Effects of Road Improvements with
      Zero Tolls   100
8-5. Direct Benefits of Road Use with Inefficient Tolls   102
8-6. Change in Dead-Weight Loss with Road Improvement   103
9-1. Bush Dweller's Alternative Responses to Discovery of
      New Path   108
9-2. Changes in Consumers' Surplus and National Income with
      Discovery of New Path   110
9-3. Comparison of National Income and Consumers' Surplus
      Benefit Measures   111
10-1. Food Supply and Demand Relationships with Costly
      Transportation   117
10-2. Variations in Land Rent and Transportation Costs with
      Distance from City   118
10-3. Effect of Road Improvement on Travel Patterns   121
10-4. Effect of Road Improvement on Land Use   122

10-5. Distribution of Transportation Improvement Benefits
Between Consumers and Land Owners   123

11-1. Effect of Manufacturing Economies of Scale and
Transportation Diseconomies of Scale on Cost
Minimizing Output Level   129

11-2. Cost Minimizing Choice of Transportation and Manufacturing
Outlays   131

12-1. Effect of Increased Road Width on Earth Moving Costs   141

12-2. Effect of Expressway Density on Number of Required Interchanges 144

12-3. Short and Long Run Cost Relationships with Economies of Scale 148

Acknowledgments

I am deeply indebted to Hayden Boyd, Richard Caves, Donald Dewey, George Douglas, Edward Foster, Ann Friedlaender, Allen Kneese, Thomas Lisco, and G. M. Neutze for the helpful substantive and editorial advice they have offered at various times during this book's long gestation process. I am also deeply indebted to Alice Jacobi for her patience, good humor, and skill in organizing the chaos I have inflicted on her into a finished manuscript. The American Economic Association, the London School of Economics and Political Science, and the University of Chicago Press have kindly granted permission to draw on articles that appeared in the *American Economic Review,* the *Journal of Transport Economics and Policy,* and the *Journal of Political Economy.*

Chapter One

Introduction: Is Transportation Different?

Transportation and Public Utilities is a well established field of specialization in economics. Two considerations seem largely responsible for this fact. First, transportation, electric power generation, and other public utilities possess institutional characteristics quite different from those of most other activities with which economists deal. The typical commodity of economics texts involves the physical transformation of materials from one form to another by people and machines located at a single point in space, while transportation entails the movement of people and things through space without (except accidentally) physical alteration. Then, too, for whatever the reasons, the state plays a much more pervasive role in transportation and public utility activities than it does in the provision of the typical textbook commodity. Through expenditures on highways, air control facilities, and the dredging and damming of waterways, and by invoking its powers of eminent domain, governmental agencies directly or indirectly provide rights-of-way for most forms of transportation. The state regulates these activities—at times in minute detail.

Second, perhaps largely because of these institutional peculiarities, the view seems prevalent that problems arise in dealing with transportation and public utilities that are qualitatively different from those treated by other branches of economics. These problems are held either to be unique in themselves or to require special tools of analysis or standards of evaluation. A few examples may be in order.

1. A great deal of attention is paid in the highway finance and public utility literature to the problem of allocating responsibility for the common costs respectively of highways and of electric power generating capacity among different user classes.[a] The general economics literature contains no com-

---

[a]See, for example, U.S. Bureau of Public Roads [8], Meyer et al. [5] (pp. 65–85), and Garfield and Lovejoy [3] (pp. 134–238). Throughout this study, text and footnote citations are to the authors of references listed in full in chapter bibliographies.

parable discussion. The conditions necessary to establish profit maximizing (and socially optimum) price and output levels for each commodity produced by a competitive, joint-product firm[b] are generally specified without reference to the average cost of producing any of them.

2. It is common in the economic development literature to find special labels such as "social overhead capital" assigned to transportation, public utility, educational, hospital, and other facilities "used by society at large, rather than by particular enterprises" (Higgins [4], p. 204). The feeling seems fairly widespread that traditional appraisal methods—essentially those that a private business firm would use in determining the value of a piece of its capital equipment—ignore the indirect effects or "external economies" of such facilities, thereby understating both their true benefits and, presumably, the socially desirable level of expenditures of them.[c]

3. If so much of a commodity is produced that expenditures on it fail to cover the costs incurred by its producers, the market for it is regarded as being in disequilibrium. Over time, resources initially devoted to its production are expected to shift to the production of other, more profitable commodities. As this shift of resources continues, the output of the unprofitable commodity declines and its price increases until revenues once again cover production costs. This process is generally deemed to be both natural and socially desirable. In the competitive world with which much of economic theory deals, preventing resources from shifting from unprofitable to profitable employments decreases the aggregate value of the goods obtainable from the limited resources at the disposal of society.

In most urban areas, the profitability of mass transit services has been decreasing steadily. In most large American cities (New York, Chicago, Philadelphia, and Boston, to cite only a few) services are maintained at their present levels only through substantial subsidies. Indeed, in many areas, major expenditures on new transit facilities are being undertaken with the full expectation that these facilities will not be self-supporting.[d] Among the most common justifications for such expenditures is the following statement:

> To make people pay what it costs is self-defeating for the reason that one of the broad social justifications of a new investment in rapid

[b]That is, a firm for which the cost incurred in producing an additional unit of one commodity depends on the rate at which one or more other commodities are being produced at the same time.

[c]As examples of this sort of reasoning applied to highway investments, see Tinbergen [7], Bos and Koyck [1], and Brown and Harral [2].

[d]In the United States as of early 1976, major improvements to existing systems in Boston, Chicago, and New York either are in process or have just been completed. An entirely new, $1.4 billion system in the San Francisco Bay Area is now in operation. New systems of comparable magnitude either are or shortly will be under construction in Atlanta, Baltimore, and Washington.

transit facilities is to relieve the urban traffic dilemma by inducing people to give up the use of private motor vehicles or to remain on public transportation if they are being discouraged by poor service. (Miller [6], p. 62).

It is with this second consideration accounting for the existence of transportation economics as a field of specialization—the putative uniqueness of the problems, analytical tools, and standards of valuation involved—that this study is primarily concerned. Its main purpose is to show that, contrary to prevailing opinion, the economist's basic theories of price and value—the tools he would use in characterizing the optimum input combinations and output levels for a dam, a steel mill, or an orange grove, or in placing a value on any of these facilities—can be employed without fundamental alteration to perform the same function for transportation activities.

To be more specific, the next two chapters show that the characteristics of both an optimum transportation system and an optimum pricing system for an existing, perhaps nonoptimum system are quite similar respectively to the characteristics of long and short run equilibrium in a competitive industry. The next nine chapters demonstrate that the external economies, which have been held to require special investment criteria for transportation and other "social overhead" facilities, have their exact counterparts in every other form of economic activity. To isolate what seem to be critical issues, the analysis of these chapters is undertaken for a fictitious world in which all markets are competitively organized and in which transportation activities are characterized by neither scale economies nor indivisibilities. Scale economies and indivisibilities are, however, very important attributes of almost all forms of transportation. The concluding chapter suggests both the nature and, to the extent that data are available, the magnitude of the most important of these scale economies and indivisibilities for various forms of transportation.

Chapter Two

Competitive Equilibrium

The characteristics of both optimum transportation systems and optimum pricing systems for them are formally quite similar to the characteristics of long and short run equilibrium in the purely competitive industries of economic theory texts. To aid in establishing this formal relationship, it seems desirable to begin by setting forth in a simple but somewhat unconventional way[a] the equilibrium relationships that would hold in a hypothetical competitive industry, widget manufacturing.

In discussing the behavior of business firms, it is common to distinguish between the "long run" and the "short run." In the short run some of the inputs used in the widget manufacturing production process are fixed. These inputs—buildings, machines, and the like—are typically referred to as "capital." A widget manufacturer can increase his use of these inputs only by placing orders that require substantial periods of time to be filled; he (or those to whom he might sell them) can decrease their use only by allowing them to wear out, an even more time-consuming process. The long run is defined as a period of time sufficiently great that the widget manufacturer can increase or decrease any or all of his productive inputs by any amount he chooses, or indeed, go out of business entirely.

That his stock of capital equipment is fixed does not necessarily mean that the manufacturer cannot vary the rate at which his factory produces widgets in the short run. A variety of means is typically available for utilizing capital equipment more or less intensively, thereby enabling output to be varied. Production can be increased, for example, by overtime work, by employing additional helpers, by operating equipment when it would normally be shut down for routine maintenance, or by being more wasteful in the use of raw materials.

Any given stock of capital equipment used in producing widgets has associated with it both average variable and short run marginal cost schedules.

[a]For a more conventional approach, see Ferguson and Gould [2] or Mansfield [3].

5

Average variable cost is obtained by dividing an expenditure on those inputs that can be varied in the short run by the maximum number of widgets[b] that expenditure can produce when employed in conjunction with the fixed stock of widget producing capital. Short run marginal cost is the increase in expenditures on variable inputs required to increase output by one unit.

Figure 2-1 depicts alternative possible relationships between output levels and these two cost concepts. In this figure, the sorts of short run marginal and average cost schedules most commonly illustrated in economics texts are shown as Type IA. Types IB and IC depict variant forms that arise in a number of transportation and public utility activities. It is usual to assume that a business firm operating in a competitive industry purchases the inputs used in its production process in competitive markets, and hence that these inputs are available at prices that are independent of the quantities used by an individual manufacturer. Given this assumption, each of the Type I schedules exhibits the "law of diminishing returns": If some inputs to a production process are held fixed while others are allowed to vary, a point exists beyond which successive equal increments of the variable inputs will add successively smaller increments to total output, or alternatively, beyond which successive equal increments to total output require successively larger expenditures on variable inputs.

For a Type IA process, this law sets in at output level A. For widget outputs of less than A, the process exhibits increasing return to the variable factors; that is, for output levels between zero and A, adding successive equal increments of variable inputs to the fixed stock of capital equipment adds successively larger increments to total output. In Types IB and IC production processes, the law of diminishing returns holds for all positive output levels. For Type IB, the law also holds for all positive input levels. Type IC, however, is peculiar in having a stage (really a point) of increasing returns to the variable factors as output goes from zero to positive.[c]

A fourth type of short run cost relationship is illustrated by Type II. A Type II cost schedule would arise in a fixed coefficient production process. That is, it would arise if, for example, one worker operating one machine and two workers operating two machines could respectively produce one and two widgets in an hour, while only one widget an hour could be produced by having either two workers operate one machine or one worker operate two machines. In such a production process, as long as some machines are idle, the

---

[b]Any given budget can be used to purchase a variety of alternative combinations of variable inputs. The input combination of relevance in drawing both average variable and short run marginal cost schedules is that which yields the maximum output of widgets per dollar spent.

[c]A highway after a severe winter blizzard offers an example of a Type IC process. Before any automobile trips can be made on it, substantial effort must be expended to clear snow from it. As will be developed, a number of common carrier transportation activities also provides examples of Type IC processes.

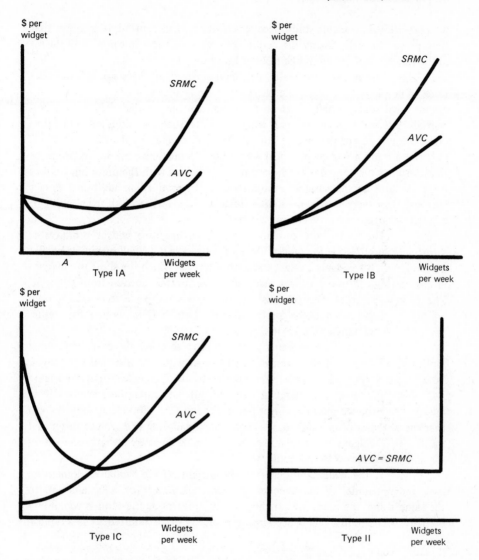

Figure 2-1.   Types of Short Run Cost Schedules

short run marginal (and average variable) cost of a widget would be the cost of employing an additional worker for one hour. Once the number of workers employed equals the number of machines available, however, there is no way in which output can be increased short of buying additional machines.

While some real-world production processes may approximate those required for Type II cost relationships, it seems reasonably safe to assert that few transportation activities are among them. Still, Type II production processes warrant attention in this study because an often unrecognized assumption that they prevail underlies many discussions of cost allocation and pricing problems in the transportation and public utilities literature.

The market for widgets is "competitive" in the sense in which the term is employed in economic theory if each manufacturer's production decisions have such a small effect on total industry output that they do not perceptibly affect the price at which widgets sell. In such a market, individual producers would accept the market price as being unaffected by their actions. Thus, in the short run a widget producer who wishes to maximize his profits produces that output which equates his short run marginal cost with the prevailing market price. As long as the variable inputs required to produce an additional widget cost less than the revenue (the market price of a widget) received from selling it, expanding output would increase profits.

The short run equilibrium of a competitive widget producer is shown in Figure 2-2. If the market price of widgets is P, he will maximize profits by producing W^* widgets a week, the output level at which the short run marginal cost of an additional widget just equals the revenue derived from selling it. The producer's total weekly sales revenue equals the price received for each widget, P, times the quantity produced, W^*. Total revenue is therefore represented by the rectangle $OPCW^*$ in Figure 2-2.

Part of these revenues must be used to cover the costs of variable inputs. At output level W^*, average variable cost would be B dollars per widget. Total variable costs are therefore represented by the rectangle $OBDW^*$ in Figure 2-2. Since the short run marginal cost schedule indicates the additional cost required to produce the first widget per week; and then the second widget, given that the first has been paid for, . . . and then finally the Wth widget, given that the W - first widget has been paid for, total variable costs are also represented by the area under the $SRMC$ schedule, $OACW^*$.

If the widget producer owns outright all the capital equipment he uses, the remainder of his revenues—the rectangle $BDCP$ (or, what amounts to the same thing, the area ACP)—is his weekly "profit" as the term is commonly used by accountants.[d] This accounting profit is often referred to as a "quasi-

---

[d]The definition of "profit" employed by accountants and in everyday conversation differs in an important respect from that commonly used by economists. According to the common definition, a firm's profit equals the difference between its total revenues and its contractual costs. Contractual costs, in turn, are the firm's outlays for hired inputs: the wages of employees, the costs of raw materials, rent on leased buildings and equipment, and interest on borrowed funds. The owners of the typical business firm supply at least some of the funds used to provide the capital equipment it employs. Under the economist's definition of profit, the return that these funds would earn if invested in government bonds, for example, is regarded as a cost of doing business. To determine profit as defined by an economist, then, it is necessary to deduct from accounting profit the value of owner-supplied assets times the rate of interest these assets would earn if employed in their most profitable alternative use—an admittedly tough concept to quantify.

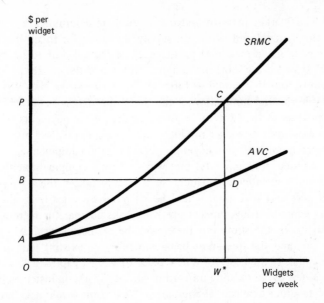

Figure 2-2. Short Run Equilibrium of a Competitive Business Firm

rent"[e] on the widget producer's capital equipment.[f] Given constant returns to scale,[g] this quasi-rent can be shown to equal the value of the marginal product of the total stock of widget-producing capital equipment. That is, it equals the amount of widget capital times the increase in the value of widget output that would result from holding all variable inputs fixed but employing a small additional amount of capital. In symbols:

$$ACP = BDCP = P \times MPK \times K \tag{2-1}$$

where P, MPK, and K refer respectively to the market price of widgets, the marginal physical product of a unit of widget-producing capital equipment, and the number of units of widget capital owned by the manufacturer.

---

[e]"Rent" in the sense of being a payment to an input that is not required to evoke its services; "quasi" in the sense that, if it earned no compensation, the services of fixed capital would be provided only until it depreciated or could in some way be transferred to another use.

[f]For simplicity, the possible existence of specialized entrepreneurial skills or other attributes of the firm to which rents might be imputed are ignored here. Again for simplicity, the assumptions that all widget manufacturers employ the same production process and pay the same prices for inputs are also implicit in what follows.

[g]That is, given a state of affairs in which multiplication of all inputs by any positive number, k, would results in a k-fold increase in output.

The market price of widgets, in turn, is determined by the intersection of the demand and short run supply schedules for them. If all widget manufacturers desire to maximize profits, each can be relied on to establish that output level at which his short run marginal cost equals the market price. Hence the aggregate output that would be forthcoming at alternative market prices can be found by horizontal summation of the short run marginal cost schedules of all widget producers. In short run equilibrium, aggregate payments to the variable inputs employed in widget products equal the area *OBDW** in Figure 2-3, while aggregate quasi-rents on widget-producing capital equipment equal *BDCP*.

Assume, for simplicity, that widget capital equipment neither wears out nor requires maintenance. Under such circumstances the cost per time period of a new unit of capital would be its purchase price times the rate of return being earned on investments involving risks comparable to those in the widget industry. In the short run there need be no necessary relationship between this cost and the quasi-rent being earned by an existing unit of widget-producing capital. If the cost[h] of a new piece of widget capital is less than the quasi-rent earned by an existing unit, firms already in the industry would have an incentive to order new capital equipment. New firms would also have an inducement to establish themselves in the industry.

As an individual widget manufacturer adds to the productive capacity of his factory, its short run marginal cost schedule shifts to the right. That is, the short run marginal cost of producing any given level of output falls and the output that would equate short run marginal cost with any given market price increases. As industry capacity increases, then, industry output will also increase and both widget prices and quasi-rents per unit of capital will decline. Long run equilibrium can be defined as having been reached when this process of capital entry and price decline has progressed to the point where any of three equivalent conditions hold: the quasi-rent earned on a unit of widget-producing capital equals its cost; no *economic* profits are being earned in the industry; and *accounting* profits[i] plus interest paid on borrowed funds equal the cost of widget capital.[j] In symbols, long run equilibrium involves the equality of all the following magnitudes:

$$BDCP \text{ (in Fig. 2-3)} = P \times MPK \times K = r \times P_K \times K \qquad (2\text{-}2)$$

[h] To emphasize, throughout this book, the phrase "cost of a unit of capital" will be used to refer to the cost per time period of using its services, and not to the purchase price of that unit.

[i] For the distinction between economic and accounting profits, see footnote *d*.

[j] Taking into account those maintenance costs of capital equipment that are independent of the level at which the equipment is used would require modifying the end of this sentence to read something like, ". . . the market return on the cost of reproducing it plus those maintenance and depreciation costs that are independent of the rate at which capital is utilized." Those maintenance and depreciation costs that do depend on the rate at which capital is utilized are among the variable inputs to the production process.

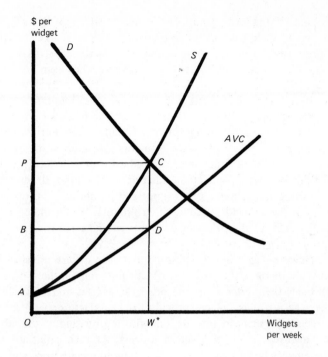

Figure 2-3. Short and Long Run Equilibrium of a Competitive Industry

where K, P_K, and r refer respectively to the aggregate stock of widget producing capital, the purchase price of a unit of capital, and the appropriate market rate of return.

Type I production processes are implicit in the way Figures 2-2 and 2-3 have been drawn. In Figure 2-2, the firm's short run marginal cost schedule slopes from southwest to northeast. A change in the price of widgets stemming from a shift in the industry demand schedule would therefore change the output level at which price equals short run marginal cost. Hence a change in the market price would lead to an immediate change in industry output.

This same conclusion does not apply if widget production involves a Type II process and if each producer experiences the same variable costs per unit of output. Under such circumstances, as long as the price of widgets exceeds the average variable (equal short run marginal) costs of producing them, each Type II producer would operate his factory at its capacity. A change in market price would have no short run effect on aggregate output. Thus for all prices above average variable cost, the short run supply schedule for such an industry would be a vertical line at an output level equal to industry capacity.

Despite the difference between the short run responses to price changes of Type I and Type II producers, the essential conclusion reached above would still hold for the latter group. If the market price of widgets differs from that which would yield quasi-rents equal to the relevant market return on the purchase price of widget capital equipment, industry capacity will change. Long run equilibrium can still be defined as existing when aggregate quasi-rents equal $r \times P_K \times K$, to use the symbols defined in equation (2-2) above.

Two further important points deserve brief mention before transportation activities are considered directly. First, the process by which a competitive industry approaches long run equilibrium is decentralized. Neither information on events elsewhere in the economy nor intervention by some outside agency is required to bring about this adjustment process. True, both the demand for the industry's product and the prices of its inputs depend at least in principle on the price of every other input and product sold in the economy. Thus changes in the demand for some other product, the technology employed in manufacturing it, or the prices of its inputs can have ramifications affecting the equilibrium price and output of widgets.

However, ignoring the possible existence of technological externalities,[k] events elsewhere in the economy affect equilibrium in the widget industry entirely through their effects on the prices of widgets and of the industry's inputs. The relevant marketplaces provide the manufacturer with information on these prices. His engineers provide him with information on the substitution possibilities involved in his production process. At each point in time, this information enables him to adjust variable inputs to equate price and short run marginal costs. If the industry is not in equilibrum at some point in time, the responses of individual producers to information on prices and production possibilities will so alter the capital and other inputs devoted to widget production that, as time progresses, the price and output of widgets approach their long run equilibrium values.[1] Again, neither information on events elsewhere in the economy nor intervention by some outside agency is required to bring about this adjustment process.

Not only is this process of adjustment decentralized, it is also socially desirable in a quite precise sense of the term. That the price of widgets

---

[k]A technological externality can be defined as existing when the number of widgets obtainable from a given bundle of those inputs purchased by the widget manufacturer depends on the input combination or output level of some other producer. Commonly cited examples of technological externalities are the effects of the amount of smoke produced by a factory on the amount of soap required to launder a pound of clothes or of the number of trips being taken on the time required to complete a trip—see Chapter Three.

[1]In light of the recent mathematical literature on the stability, uniqueness, and indeed existence of competitive equilibrium, this is much too sweeping an assertion. To be more nearly correct, this sentence should have been preceded by a phrase such as, "If the nature of production processes, the ways in which producers adjust to changing market conditions, and the character of aggregate consumer preferences satisfy some quite restrictive conditions . . .". For a lucid, elementray discussion of the literature on activity analysis and general equilibrium see Baumol [1], ch. 21.

(or of any other commodity) equals the marginal (social—and again, external-ities are being ignored) cost of producing them is a necessary condition for an optimum organization of economic activity. That is, if price does *not* equal marginal cost in all markets it would be possible, by changing the output levels of some commodities, to improve the welfare of some individual or group with-out at the same time harming any other individual or group. Why this conclusion holds can perhaps most easily be seen by exploring the consequences for the remainder of the economy of a change in widget output from its competitive equilibrium level.

In a free enterprise economy, resources are valued according to their ability to produce goods and services that are desired by consumers. If the market value of the added output that would result from employing an addi-tional unit of some resource in a production process exceeds the unit price of that resource, a producer would increase his profits by employing more of it. Similarly, a consumer would benefit from buying additional units of a com-modity if its market price is less than he would be willing to pay for them.[m] Thus the workings of each market in a competitive economy can be relied upon to equate what some consumer would just be willing to pay for an additional unit of the commodity in question with the market value of the resources that enter into its production.

Suppose that such a state of equilibrium had been reached in all the markets in a competitive economy, including that for widgets. In addition, suppose that society collectively decided to increase widget ouptut. Doing so would require shifting resources from other activities to the production of widgets, thereby decreasing the output of these other goods by an amount equiv-alent to the market value of the shifted resources. However, to sell the added output of widgets would require decreasing their price to below the present equilibrium level and hence to below the market value of the goods the shifted resources could have produced. As a result of this shift, society would reap additional benefits from its added widget consumption. However, this gain would be more than offset by the loss in benefits resulting from the decreased production of other goods and services.

That the responses of consumers and business firms to the product and input prices determined in the decentralized markets of a competitive economy optimize the organization of economic activity does not, it should hastily be added, constitute complete justification for an economic policy of laissez-faire. Externalities and noncompetitive elements exist in many markets.

---

[m]More precisely, if the additional satisfaction a consumer derives from spend-ing an additional dollar on commodity X exceeds the additional satisfaction he derives from spending the dollar on commodity Y, he would benefit by increasing his expenditures on X and decreasing them on Y. To maximize the satisfaction he derives from his limited income, a consumer must adjust his expenditures so as to equalize the additional satisfaction that would result from spending an additional dollar on any commodity.

And even if this were not the case, society might well feel that the market rewards to some of its members are intolerably high or low. If so, society would presumably wish to reallocate income in a fashion that it feels to be more equitable. Income redistribution and efficiency are not incompatible, however. It would be possible, at least in principle, to redistribute income while still continuing to allocate resources optimally.[n]

What competitive equilibrium theory does suggest in this connection is that proposals to subsidize particular activities should be evaluated skeptically. Justifications for subsidies do arise in competitive equilibrium theory when indivisibilities, scale economies, or technological externalities are present. (Subsidy justifications and their applications to transportation activities are discussed in later chapters.) These economic arguments are infrequently employed by subsidy proponents, however. Rather, their advocacy typically rests exclusively on the putative benefits to society at large or to some worthy group that would result from the increased output of the subsidized commodity. Such arguments almost invariably overlook the opportunity costs of the resources involved. They are therefore highly suspect.

[n]The postredistribution optimum would, of course, be different from that which would prevail under laissez-faire. As such, economic theory can provide no clues as to which of the infinite number of possible optimum allocations of resources would be best for society. All it can do in this connection is point out that, if an optimum resource allocation has not been achieved, it would be possible to make someone better off without harming anyone else.

Chapter Three

Congestion and the Optimization of Transportation Activities

Transportation is unusual (although by no means unique) among economic activities in that those who use transportation services play both a consuming and a producing role. To take a trip or to ship goods involves not only the purchase of a service but also the provision of at least one input vital to its production: the time of the traveler or that of his goods. Taking the producing role of transportation consumers directly into account can greatly simplify the analysis of transportation problems. It can do so by making it possible to deal with these problems by applying, without appreciable alteration, the analysis in Chapter Two of short and long run equilibrium in the competitively organized widget industry. The validity of this assertion can perhaps most easily be established by beginning with a discussion of the congestion phenomenon.

While "congestion" is a term most commonly applied to traffic on city streets, the concept can usefully be generalized. Congestion can be defined as affecting activities in which (1) buyers supply some of the variable inputs— most commonly their own time or that of commodities they own—required to produce goods or services, and (2) the required quantity of these inputs per unit of output or the quality of the product itself depend on the rate at which purchases are made.

When defined in this way, congestion can be seen to be a factor in a wide range of economic activities. For example, shopping probably occupies more of the average householder's time than any other single nonwork activity. The wait for service in a department store is typically substantially longer during the week before Christmas than in late January. Similarly, the length of the queue at a super market checkout counter and hence the time spent in it is normally longer on Saturday than during the remainder of the week. As for the quality of product dimension of congestion, an increase in the number of customers attending a movie performance is typically associated with a decrease in the odds of finding a seat with an undistorted or otherwise unencumbered view of the screen.

Congestion clearly plays a role in most transportation activities. Some highway maintenance costs are affected by the rate at which a highway is used, particularly when studded snow tires and overloaded trucks are involved. Apart from these costs, however, all the variable inputs—gasoline, oil, tire wear, and travel time—required for private passenger vehicle trips are supplied by travelers themselves. According to the American Association of State Highway Officials "Red Book" [3], gasoline consumption and other vehicle operating costs on rural highways and urban expressways depend only on the speed at which a driver desires to travel, not on the speed which prevailing traffic conditions allow him to attain. That is, on such highways, vehicle operating costs appear to be independent of traffic volume.[a] When traffic is light, drivers are able to attain their desired speeds. However, as traffic density increases, so too does the number of passing maneuvers required to maintain all but the slowest speeds. At the same time, the frequency with which these maneuvers can be performed decreases, and as a result, average realized speeds decrease with increases in traffic density. This fact suggests that adding a vehicle to a traffic stream involves costs not only for the operator of the additional vehicle but also for every other vehicle in the traffic stream in the form of a reduction in their realized speeds.

The highway literature reports a number of attempts to establish empirical relations between travel time and traffic density. In general, these relationships take the form:

$$T = f(N/K)$$

where N denotes traffic volume (i.e., the actual number of trips taken per hour on a stretch of road), K is the capacity of that stretch (i.e., the maximum number of trips per hour that could be taken on it), and T is the average time required to travel a mile.

Perhaps the simplest of these empirical relationships, one derived from an analysis by Coleman [1] of data on city street traffic, can be written:

$$T = 5.67 - 3.33 (1 - N/K)^{\frac{1}{2}}$$

---

[a]At least above 20–25 miles per hour, gasoline consumption and other vehicle operating costs increase with increases in the sustained speed at which a vehicle travels. Increases in traffic density are associated with declines in average speeds, and, for that reason alone, with decreased operating costs. At the same time, however, as traffic density increases, the average driver finds it increasingly necessary alternatively to decelerate as he approaches slow vehicles and to accelerate as he passes them. The resulting increase in the variability of speed tends to increase operating costs. According to the "Red Book," these two opposing effects almost exactly offset each other.

Table 3-1. Average and Marginal Travel Time per Vehicle Mile on City Streets at Alternative Volume-Capacity Ratios

Volume-Capacity Ratio	Travel Time (Minutes per Mile)	
	Average	*Marginal*
0.1	2.51	2.68
0.2	2.68	3.04
0.3	2.87	3.45
0.4	3.07	3.90
0.5	3.28	4.42
0.6	3.52	5.05
0.7	3.80	5.85
0.8	4.12	6.98
0.95	4.93	12.02

Two important features of this relationship[b] warrant mention. First, it implies that the law of diminishing returns holds for the variable input, travel time, at all positive traffic volumes—that is, as the number of trips being taken on a given street increases, the number of *additional* minutes required to produce an *additional* trip steadily increases. Second, it indicates that a given street does indeed have a "capacity," in the sense of being able to produce trips at a rate no greater than some specifiable maximum. If the rate at which travelers attempt to make trips exceeds this capacity level, travel time per trip will continue to increase. However, the number of trips actually completed will fall.

The travel times per vehicle mile implied by the Coleman relationship at alternative volume-capacity (N/K) ratios are listed in the first column of Table 3-1. Marginal travel time per vehicle mile can reasonably be defined as the number of minutes an additional trip taker would require to travel one mile plus the number of minutes this additional trip adds to the time required for the trips of all other travelers by reducing their attainable speeds. Marginal travel times per vehicle mile at alternative volume-capacity ratios can be determined by appropriately manipulating the Coleman relationship.[c] These values are shown in the second column of Table 3-1. As they indicate, travel time costs increase substantially with increases in the rate at which a street is utilized. Further, the difference between marginal and average values is substantial, particularly at high volume-capacity ratios.

[b]And, for that matter, virtually every other relationship between travel time and volume-capacity ratios that has been reported in the literature. For a discussion of some of these relationships, see Mohring [2].

[c]If travel time per mile is given by the Coleman relationship, then the *total* travel time required to make N one-mile trips per hour is $NT = N[5.67 - 3.33(1 - N/K)^{1/2}]$. Differentiating this relationship with respect to N yields $d(NT)/dN = T + (1.67 N/K)/(1 - N/K)^{1/2}$ as marginal travel time per trip mile.

To repeat, the fact that the marginal travel time per vehicle mile is greater than the average travel time at any given volume-capacity ratio reflects the fact that the addition of a vehicle to a traffic stream imposes a definite, if small, cost on those who occupy each of the other vehicles in that stream. Suppose that the volume-capacity ratio at each point on a ten-mile-long city street is 0.5. Assuming one passenger per vehicle, the addition during any hour of one more vehicle trip along the full length of the street would then increase total travel time by an aggregate of approximately 44.2 minutes. The added trip would itself account for 32.8 minutes of this total. The remaining 11.4 minutes is the result of decreased average speeds realized by the remaining vehicles.

To put it differently, if one of the present travelers could be induced *not* to make a ten-mile trip, he would reduce the travel time of the remaining drivers by an aggregate of approximately 11.4 minutes. Suppose that this one driver had been almost indifferent about making his trip. To be specific, suppose he knew that, under prevailing travel conditions, his ten-mile trip would require 32.8 minutes and, in addition, that he would not have taken the trip if it would have required more than 35 minutes. By making a journey on which he placed a net value of, so to speak, 2.2 minutes' worth of travel time, this hypothetical driver imposes 11.4 minutes in travel time costs on the remaining drivers. Unless his time is extremely valuable, his trip would seem socially undesirable.

More generally, assume that each traveler places the same value on his travel time. It would then seem socially undesirable for anyone to make a ten-mile trip with a net value to him of less than the costs (11.4 minutes of travel time) his trip would impose on other drivers. In deciding whether to take a trip, of course, most drivers consider only the costs they bear, not those they impose on other drivers. However, if the government authority responsible for providing the highway were to levy a toll on each driver equivalent to the travel time costs his trip imposes on other drivers, socially undesirable trips would be discouraged.

The dollar amount of this "Pareto optimal" or "efficient" or "benefit maximizing" or "marginal cost" toll for ten-mile trips would depend, of course, on the value vehicle occupants place on their time—a subject discussed in Chapter Five. If, as the "Red Book" suggests (p. 126), $1.55 an hour is the value that occupants of the average vehicle place on this time, the appropriate toll for a ten-mile trip would be 29.5 cents at a volume-capacity ratio of 0.5. A higher toll would discourage trips valued at more than their full social costs by those who would otherwise take them. A lower toll would encourage trips having social costs greater than the private benefits they yield.

Figure 3-1 depicts the optimum toll and traffic levels for a city street under the assumptions that travel time is valued at $1.55 an hour, that the Coleman travel time–volume-capacity relationship holds, and that street maintenance and vehicle operating costs are independent of the level at which the

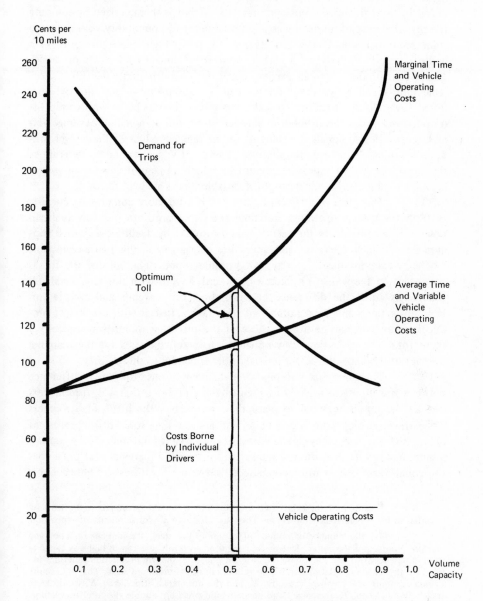

Figure 3-1. Marginal and Average Costs of City Street Trips

highway is used.[d] Comparing this diagram and Figure 2-3 is very much in order. In both figures the optimum level of output is characterized by equating the marginal cost of producing an additional unit of a commodity with the price some consumer would be willing to pay for it. In Figure 2-3, the price of a widget consists entirely of a certain number of dollars paid to its producer. The widget producer's total revenues cover both what he must pay for his variable inputs and a quasi-rent on his capital equipment. As has already been noted, given constant returns to scale, this quasi-rent can be shown to equal his output level times the difference between short run marginal and average variable costs. It also equals the value of the marginal product of the widget producer's capital equipment—the number of units of widget capital he owns times the price of a widget times the amount by which a one-unit increase in widget capital would increase widget output if variable inputs are held fixed.

The price of a trip in Figure 3-1 is a bit more complex. It consists of both the vehicle operating and time costs that are born by individual trip takers and a toll paid to the agency which provides the facility over which trips are taken. Vehicle operating and time costs play a role in this figure equivalent to the widget producer's outlays on variable inputs. The role of the toll is equivalent to the widget producer's quasi-rent. Just as with this rent, total toll collections equal the difference between short run marginal and average variable costs times the total number of trips taken. Just as with the widget producer, given constant returns to scale in the provision of highway capacity,[e] these total toll collections can be shown to equal the value of the marginal product of this capacity—a fact proved in the appendix to this chapter.

To summarize in somewhat different terms: the major difference between the situations underlying Figures 2-3 and 3-1 is that widget producers hire all the inputs required to place their product in the hands of consumers while travelers play both a producing and a consuming role. In the process of taking highway trips, they provide most of the variable (and some of the capital) inputs required. Hence, the toll required to establish a marginal cost price does not equal a trip's short run marginal cost but rather the difference between this

[d]Neither of these last two assumptions, it should be noted, is the least bit essential to the conclusions being drawn. They are adopted only for simplicity in exposition.

[e]If the number of pounds of concrete and steel, the number of labor and machine hours, and the square feet of land required to produce a unit of highway capacity were independent of the size of the highway in question, the trip production functions implied by the Coleman relationship would reflect constant returns to scale. That is, a simultaneous doubling of highway capacity, K, and the number of trips taken, N, would leave travel time *per trip, T*, unchanged and hence would precisely double the total travel time. Fortunately, or unfortunately as the case may be, the input quantities required to provide a unit of highway capacity do seem to depend on the size of the highway. As will be developed at greater length in Chapter Twelve, fairly substantial economies of scale seem to be involved in the production of highway capacity. That is, doubling the inputs employed in a particular highway would more than double its capacity.

magnitude and the variable costs born by the trip taker. Despite this difference, however, equilibrium in the production of both widgets and trips can be characterized in what are, in all vital respects, the same terms. In both situations, short run marginal cost pricing is essential to achieving Pareto optimality; and in both situations the short run marginal cost price includes a quasi-rent on invested capital equal (given constant returns to scale) to the value of its marginal product.

The similarity of equilibrium in widget production and in the provision of trips also extends to the long run. Just as in the production of widgets, in the short run the quasi-rent on capital invested in a street or highway need not equal the relevant market return on the costs of reproducing the facility. Just as with constant returns to scale widget production, long run equilibrium for a constant returns highway can be defined as having been reached when the capitalized value of the quasi-rents earned by the highway equals the cost of reproducing it.

Thus, setting marginal cost prices for highway trips and, more generally, transportation services is not necessarily incompatible with having a self-supporting system. Given constant returns to scale, employment of two quite simple operating rules would lead to both a Pareto optimal utilization of an existing (perhaps nonoptimum) transportation network and, ultimately, a long run optimum network. These rules are: (1) Establish short run marginal cost prices for the use of each link in an existing network. Doing so would require levying tolls equal to the difference between the short run marginal and average variable costs of trips. And (2) alter the size of each link to the point where the toll revenues generated by it equal the costs to the authority of providing that link, i.e., maintenance and other operating costs, depreciation, and imputed interest on invested capital.

The Relationships Among Congestion Tolls, Capacity Costs, and the Value of the Marginal Product of Capacity

If the production of trips on a highway involves constant returns to scale, travel time per trip can be written as a function of the volume-capacity ratio, N/K, and the cost of capacity can be written as $r P_K K$. Ignoring vehicle operating costs for simplicity and denoting the average value of an hour's time by V, the total variable costs of all the trips taken during a particular time period can be written

$$C = VNT = VNf(N/K) \qquad (3-1)$$

The short run marginal cost of a trip is

$$\partial C/\partial N = Vf(N/K) + VNf'[\partial(N/K)/\partial N] = Vf(N/K) + Vf' N/K$$

$$(3-2)$$

The first term on the right of equation (3-2) is the average time cost per trip; the second is the difference between the average and the marginal time cost of a trip. To set the price of a trip equal to its marginal cost, a toll equal to this latter magnitude would have to be charged each of the N travelers. If this were done, total toll collections would be $Vf' N^2/K$.

The marginal product of any input equals the change in output resulting from employment of an additional unit of that input while holding other inputs fixed. An expression for the marginal product of capacity can be found by differentiating equation (3-1) with respect to K and setting the result equal to zero, thereby indicating that variable inputs. $Nt = C/V$, are being held fixed:

$$\partial C/\partial K = Vf(N/K)dN/dK + VNf'[KdN/dK - N]/K^2 = 0 \qquad (3-3)$$

Equation (3-3) can be rearranged to give

$$K[Vf(N/K) + Vf' N/K] \, dN/dK = Vf' N^2/K \tag{3-4}$$

In equation (3-4), dN/dK is the marginal product of highway capacity. The expression in brackets by which it is multiplied equals the price of a trip *if* a toll equal to the difference between the marginal and average variable costs of a trip is levied. Hence, the left-hand side of this equation gives the value of the marginal product of K units of highway capacity, while the right-hand side equals total toll collections. Dividing equation (3-4) through by K leads to the conclusion that the value of the marginal product of a unit of capacity equals N/K times the efficient congestion toll for a single trip. This conclusion holds regardless of the number of units of capacity employed.

The total costs of N trips can be written

$$TC = VNf(N/K) + rP_K K \tag{3-5}$$

To determine the cost minimizing level of capacity requires differentiating equation (3-5) with respect to K and setting the result equal to zero. Performing this differentiation and multiplying the result through by K yields

$$rP_K K^* = Vf' N^2/K^* \tag{3-6}$$

where K^* is the cost minimizing value of K. The left-hand side of this expression is the cost of K^* units of capacity while the right-hand side equals total toll collections from setting the price of each trip on the road equal to its marginal cost.

Chapter Four

Differences in Travel Time Values and the Optimization of Transportation Facilities

Transportation—as well as other activities in which congestion plays a part—is, to repeat, different from typical textbook commodities in that consumers play a dual role. Travelers and shippers both consume a service and provide at least one of the inputs vital to its production—their own time or that of the goods they ship. The value of these consumer supplied inputs often bulks large in the total cost of transportation services. For example, Figure 3-1 indicated the marginal cost of a ten-mile trip on a representative urban street to be $1.39 at a volume-capacity ratio of 0.5. Of this total, 18 percent represents vehicle operating costs, 61 percent reflects the time costs borne by individual drivers, and the remaining 21 percent is the gap between marginal and average variable costs.

This gap arises because each vehicle trip imposes time costs on all other travelers by reducing attainable speeds. Thus, the cost components that either directly or indirectly reflect the value of travel time account for more than 80 percent of the marginal cost price shown in Figure 3-1.

This proportion does reflect a substantial element of arbitrariness, it should be added. The conversion of minutes into dollars underlying Figure 3-1 was based on a total value of $1.55 an hour for the travel time of the 1.8 occupants of the average private passenger vehicle. In presenting this value in 1960, the authors of the AASHO "Red Book" [4] suggest it to have been drawn out of a hat: "A value of travel time for passenger cars of $1.55 per hour, or 2.59 cents per minute, is used herein as representative of current opinion for a logical and practical value" (pp. 103-104).[a] Still, as long as an average value of more than 35 cents an hour is attached to private passenger vehicle time, it would account directly or indirectly for more than half the marginal cost of

---

[a]The 1960 value of $1.55 an hour is misleadingly precise. It appears to have been obtained by adjusting a 1949 estimate of $1.00 an hour to reflect price and income increases during the subsequent eleven years.

a trip on a representative city street at a volume-capacity ratio of 0.5. And, at a volume-capacity ratio of 0.9, a value of as little as 16.5 cents per vehicle hour would suffice to make travel time account for more than half this cost.

In brief, travel time is an important—perhaps dominant—input for automobile travel and many other transportation activities. Hence, it is particularly important to obtain answers to two questions: First, at what dollar magnitudes are various types of travel time valued? An accurate answer to this question is essential if transportation facilities are to be designed and priced efficiently. Clearly the characteristics of a road required to minimize the sum of the costs of the inputs supplied by transportation agencies and users would be different if users value their time at ten cents an hour than if they value it at ten dollars an hour.

Second, on most transportation facilities, individual users differ substantially in the values they attach to their travel time. A millionaire would likely pay more to save a minute's travel time than would an unemployed ditch digger using the same expressway. In this respect, transportation activities differ significantly from the more usually considered commodities. If it costs one manufacturer ten cents to produce a widget and another ten dollars, the high cost producer will soon retire from production. But if a millionaire wishes to travel from Here to There, he must do it himself—he cannot employ a ditch digger to perform the service for him. Might not this difference between transportation and widgets make the competitive equilibrium analogy developed in Chapter Three inapplicable to transportation activities?

Procedures for estimating the value of travel time and the results of applying these procedures are the subject of Chapter Five. As for the second of these questions, consider the following example of what, at least at first glance, seems to be among the most plausible of the common arguments for subsidizing mass transit systems.

> To make people pay what it costs is self-defeating for the reason that one of the broad social justifications of a new investment in rapid transit facilities is to relieve the urban traffic dilemma by inducing people to give up the use of private motor vehicles or to remain on public transportation if they are being discouraged by poor service (Miller [1], p. 62).

These and similar statements seem to contend that some automobile drivers (or the public at large) ought to be willing to subsidize, to bribe, other automobile drivers to switch to transit because those left driving automobiles would benefit from the resulting reduction in highway congestion. Put in these terms, the argument loses some of its initial appeal. After all, an analogous argument could be applied to any other pair of substitute commodities. For example, a shift from orange to apple consumption would, at least in the short run, reduce orange prices and increase apple prices. As a result, both apple producers and the remaining orange consumers would gain. Both groups therefore ought to be willing to offer bribes to encourage the shift. At the same time, however, both orange producers and apple consumers would suffer from the shift and therefore would be willing to offer at least partially offsetting bribes. The two sets of potential bribes would in fact exactly offset each other—if both orange and apple markets are initially in long run competitive equilibrium.

At least some of the same considerations apply to the markets for automobile and mass transit trips. While automobile drivers and transit operators would, at least in the short run, benefit from a shift away from automobile transportation, present users of public conveyances would likely suffer. Buses and subways would become more crowded and the duration and number of stops would likely increase. Thus, just as in competitive apple and orange markets, bribes to take and to avoid taking mass transit would tend to cancel each other out.

There is at least one peculiarity of transportation activities that suggests the orange-apple analogy to be inapplicable.[b] Contrary to one of the implicit assumptions underlying the analysis of Chapter Three, the value of travel time quite likely varies substantially among travelers. This presumed fact would pose no problems if neither indivisibilities nor scale economies were involved in the provision of transportation facilities. Under such circumstances each origin-destination pair could be provided with separate facilities for each travel time valuation class. The analysis of the preceding section would then apply to each of these facilities.

Mere mention of this possibility makes its impracticality apparent. Indivisibilities abound in the provision of transportation facilities. Each railroad track must have two rails and each road must be at least as wide as the vehicles that use it. Producers of trips having widely different costs therefore normally utilize any given transportaiton facility. That the occupant of one vehicle values his time at fifty dollars an hour and the occupant of another at ten cents might well seem to make the orange-apple analogy inapplicable. That is, this presumed fact might seem to open the way to mutually beneficial and socially desirable bribes even if both public and private transportaiton are in the equivalent of long run competitive equilibrium.

As it turns out, recognition of the fact that individual travelers differ in the values they place on their travel time does *not* require altering the conclusions reached in Chapter Three in dealing with either a single transportation facility or a group of facilities that provide similar services. Unfortunately, I have been unable to devise a rigorous way of demonstrating this fact that does

---

[b]Another, the existence of substantial scale economies in the provision of mass transit services, is discussed in Chapter twelve.

not require rather messy mathematics. As a first step in suggesting how this conclusion can be reached, the Appendix to this chapter provides a formal demonstration of propositions that can be expressed in the following terms:

1. Suppose that an individual enjoys consuming two normal commodities, *a* and *c,* and also enjoys what happens There during each of the *b* round trips per week he takes by bus between Here and There. However, he gets *dis*utility from the time he actually spends aboard the bus. The consumer will then maximize the satisfaction he derives from the limited income at his disposal by adjusting his expenditures on these commodities to satisfy

$$muc/mua = P_c/P_a \tag{4-1}$$

$$mub/mua = (F + Vt)/P_a \tag{4-2}$$

In these expressions, *mua* and *muc* refer respectively to the marginal or additional utility the consumer would derive from consuming an additional unit of *a* and *c*, while *mub* is the additional utility afforded by an additional visit to There. P_a and P_c are the market prices of commodities *a* and *c*. *F* and *t* are respectively the fare charged for a bus round trip and the time that trip requires. *V* can be interpreted as the consumer's (marginal) value of travel time—the rate at which he would be willing to reduce his consumption of *a* in return for a reduction in the travel time involved in a Here-There round trip. What equations (4-1) and (4-2) say, then, is that $F + Vt$ plays a role in the consumer's trip-making decision process identical to that played by the prices, P_a and P_b, in his decisions regarding consumption of the more normally considered commodities. For this reason, $F + Vt$ will henceforth be referred to as the "full price of a trip."

2. If the users of an existing transportation facility place different values on their travel time, to utilize the facility efficiently requires that the same toll be charged as would be efficient if each of the same number of users place a value on their time equal to the weighted (by number of trips taken) average of the time values of those who actually do use the facility. The same consideration applies to determining optimum characteristics for a new facility. The value of time entering into the optimization calculations should be the weighted average of the time values of its potential users.

That recognition of differences in travel time values does not require altering the conclusions of Chapter Three can perhaps be made more plausible by considering some simple examples. Suppose that 1,000 people per hour drive between Here and There. Travel time is the only cost of their trips. The values they place on time are uniformly distributed between zero and $12.00 an hour or, what amounts to the same thing, between zero and 20 cents a minute.[c] To begin with, suppose that it is possible to build only one expressway between the two cities. Travel time per mile (*t*) on the expressway is given by a variant of the Coleman travel time–volume-capacity relationship described in Chapter Three:

$$t = 2 - (1 - N/K)^{\frac{1}{2}} \tag{4-3}$$

This relationship says that at a volume-capacity (N/K) ratio of zero, travel time is one minute per mile, a speed of 60 miles per hour. The relationship also says that, at a volume-capacity ratio of one, travel speed is 30 miles per hour.

Suppose that, regardless of freeway size, a unit of rural freeway capacity costs one cent per mile per hour.[d] The authority responsible for providing the freeway desires to minimize the sum of the capital and the time costs of trips, and at the same time to make the highway exactly self-supporting. That is, it plans to levy tolls on drivers just sufficient to cover the total capital costs of the road.

In seeking to minimize the total cost of trips, the highway authority can exercise control over only one variable, highway capacity (*K*). An increase in the number of units of capacity it provides will reduce the volume-capacity ratio and hence the time cost of trips but will, at the same time, increase the capital cost of the highway. Total costs would therefore be a minimum if capacity is increased to the point where the additional capital cost incurred through adding one more unit of capacity is exactly offset by the reduction in travel time costs to which that increase in capacity gives rise. Establishing this relationship between capital cost increases and travel time cost savings would involve equating the value of the marginal product of capital with its marginal cost, to use the terminology of Chapter Two. With such an equality established, Chapter Three indicates that the revenue generated by charging each driver a toll equal to the difference between short run marginal and average variable

[c]That is, no driver places either a negative value or a value in excess of 20 cents a minute on his time; 50 drivers an hour value their time at between zero and 1 cent a minute, 50 drivers at 1–2 cents a minute, and so forth.

[d]This number is based on an assumed capital cost for a four-lane expressway of a million dollars a mile. If the capacity of a lane is 1,800 vehicles per hour and if an interest rate of 10 percent is appropriate to valuing highway investments, an hourly capital cost per unit of capacity of 0.27 cents per mile is implied. The remaining 0.73 cents roughly reflects maintenance, depreciation, snow plowing, policing, and other current costs of operating the expressway.

costs would, given constant returns to scale, exactly cover the capital costs of the highway.

The average value ot travel time (V) for all drivers between Here and There is ten cents per minute. The total hourly cost (in cents per mile) of trips can therefore be written

$$C = VNt + K = 10 \cdot 1{,}000 \cdot [2 - (1 - 1{,}000/K)^{\frac{1}{2}}] + K \qquad (4\text{-}4)$$

The value of K which minimizes this expression can be found by trial and error methods.[e] It turns out to be 2536. Thus, at one cent per mile of capacity, the hourly cost of an optimum size highway would be $25.36 per mile. Dividing the cost of the optimum size highway by 1,000 travelers per hour yields 2.536 cents per mile. If time per trip mile is given by equation (4-3) and if the average over all drivers of the value of one minute's travel time is V, the toll per mile required to equate the cost borne by an individual driver with the marginal time cost of his trip—the gap between short run marginal and average variable costs—can be shown[f] to be

$$T = VN/[2K(1 - N/K)^{\frac{1}{2}}] \qquad (4\text{-}5)$$

On substituting ten cents per minute for V, 1,000 for N, and 2,536 for K in equation (4-5), T works out to be 2.536 cents per mile—precisely the amount required to make the highway self-supporting.

The same sort of consideration carries over in dealing with more than one transportation facility. Suppose that, instead of a single highway, the public authority finds it possible to construct two roads between Here and There, each characterized by the capital cost and travel time–volume-capacity relationship given above for the single road. Minimizing the total cost of trips on this two-road system would require that one road be restricted to those drivers who place the lowest values on their travel time. Trips on this road would involve a relatively high travel time but a relatively low capital cost per trip mile. The second road, more lavish in terms of volume-capacity ratios, would then be used by those travelers who place the highest values on their travel time. Drivers could be segregated in this fashion by decree or, alternatively, by charging different tolls for use of the two roads.

Regarding this latter possibility, let T_s and T_f respectively denote the tolls per mile on the slow and fast roads, and let t_s and t_f indicate the associated travel times per minute. Then traveler i, who places a value of V_i on

[e]Or, alternatively, by noting that $dC/dK = 0$ implies, after rearranging terms, $K^4 - 1000 K^3 - 25 \cdot 10^{12} = 0$. The positive root of this equation can be determined by iterative techniques.

[f]By differentiating total time cost, $NVt = NV[2 - (1 - N/K)^{\frac{1}{2}}]$, with respect to N and subtracting the average time cost per trip, Vt, from the result.

his travel time, is confronted by two full prices of trip miles between Here and There: $T_s + V_i t_s$ and $T_f + V_i t_f$ on the slow and fast roads respectively. He will presumably choose to travel on that road which involves the lower of these two full prices. Suppose that $T_s + V_i t_s > T_f + V_i t_f$, i.e., that the time saved on the fast road is, to him, more than worth the additional toll it entails. Re-arranging terms yields, $V_i > (T_f - T_s)/(t_s - t_f)$. The right-hand side of this expression can be interpreted as the price the traveler must pay to save one minute's travel time by using the fast road. He and all other drivers who value their time at more than this price would use the fast road; the remainder would take the slow road.

In seeking to minimize the total cost of trips, then, the highway authority can exercise control over three variables: the capacities of the two roads, K_s and K_f, and, by manipulating the toll differential, the number of drivers per hour using the slow road, N_s, and hence the number using the fast road, $N_f = 1,000 - N_s$. Minimizing total costs would require each of two sorts of relationships to be put into effect simultaneously. First, for any given allocation of travelers between the two roads, K_s and K_f must be selected so as to minimize the equivalents of equation (4-4), the total cost of trips taken on each road. That is, the capacity of each road must be set so as to equate the value of its marginal product with its marginal cost. Second, given a pair of capacities for the two roads, travelers must be shifted from, say, the fast road to the slow road to the point where, for the last traveler shifted, the additional slow road costs incurred are just offset by the resulting saving in fast road costs.

The additional slow road costs are of two sorts. First, the shifted traveler goes at a slower speed. He therefore directly incurs higher time costs. Second, he adds to congestion on the slow road and hence to the travel costs of its other users. Offsetting these effects, his shift lowers fast road costs by reducing congestion and hence travel time costs on it. If drivers are ranked in ascending order of their travel time valuations, the slow road user who places the highest value on his travel time, driver N_s, would value it at $20 \times N_s/1,000 = N_s/50$ cents per minute. The average travel time of *all* slow road users, V_s, would be just one half this amount, $N_s/100$ cents per minute. The average value of time for fast road drivers would be midway between that of driver N_s and 20 cents per minute, the highest value placed on his time by any driver. That is, V_f would equal $(N_s/50 + 20)/2$ or $10 + N_s/100$ cents per mile.

The total hourly cost of trips is the sum of their time costs plus the hourly capital costs of the two roads:

$$C = K_s + K_f + N_s V_s t_s + N_f V_f t_f$$

$$= K_s + K_f + N_s (N_s/100) [2 - (1 - N_s/K_s)^{1/2}]$$

$$+ (1,000 - N_s)(10 + N_s/100) [2 - (1 - N_f/K_f)^{1/2}] \qquad (4\text{-}6)$$

As with the one road case, the cost minimizing values of K_s, K_f, N_s, and hence N_f can be found by trial and error methods, albeit with considerably greater difficulty.[g] They turn out to be $K_s = 561$, $K_f = 1,899$, $N_s = 341$, and hence $N_f = 1,000 - 341 = 659$. At one cent each, the hourly cost of the 561 units of slow road capacity would be \$5.61 per mile. The toll per trip mile required to make the slow road exactly self-supporting would therefore be \$5.61/341 per traveler or 1.648 cents. Similarly, the toll per mile required to make the fast road self-supporting would be \$18.99/659 or 2.880 cents. If 341 drivers use it, the average travel time value on the slow road would be 341/100 = 3.41 cents per minute, while the corresponding average for the fast road would be 13.41 cents per minute.

Substituting these numbers in equation (4-5), together with those for the cost minimizing numbers of users and levels of capacity, yields 1.648 and 2.880 cents as the tolls per trip mile required to equate the time cost borne by individual slow and fast road drivers with the marginal time costs of their trips. But these tolls, note, are precisely those that would be required to make each of the two roads exactly self-supporting. In addition, by substituting 341 for N and 561 for K in equation (4-3), it can be found that it would take 1.373 minutes to travel one mile on the slow road. Performing this substitution for the fast road yields a travel time per mile of 1.192 minutes. Hence the travel time of the last traveler shifted from the fast to the slow road, driver 341, is increased by 0.181 minutes per mile by the shift. Since he values his time at 341/50 = 6.82 cents per minute, the direct increase in his travel costs is 6.82 × 0.181 = 1.232 cents per mile.

The additional costs his shift imposes on slow road drivers equals the toll for a slow road trip, 1.648 cents per mile. Similarly, the saving to fast road drivers equals the toll for a trip on that road, 2.880 cents per mile. Hence the net effect of his shift is 1.232 + 1.648 − 2.880 = 0 cents per mile. Furthermore, since the difference between slow and fast road tolls is 1.232 cents per mile and the difference in travel times on the two roads is 0.181 minutes per mile, 1.232/0.181 = 6.82 cents per minute—the cost of saving time by using the fast road. But note: this is precisely the value driver 341 attaches to his time.

In brief, at least for this simple highway network, the conclusions reached in Chapters Two and Three still hold when differences among drivers in travel time values are recognized. Suppose that providing highway capacity involves constant returns to scale and that the highway system is designed to minimize the total costs of trips between Here and There. Then charging each user of each highway the toll required to equate the time costs he bears with the short run marginal costs of his trips would do three important things: First, it would make him take into account the costs his trips impose on other travelers;

[g]These values were actually determined by using an iterative technique to solve the first order conditions for cost minimization, $\partial C/\partial K_s = \partial C/\partial K_f = \partial C/\partial N_s = 0$.

second, such tolls would suffice to make each road in the highway system exactly self-supporting; and third, these tolls would induce travelers to distribute themselves between the two roads in an efficient fashion. In other words, the difference between slow and fast road tolls and travel times would lead each traveler to select that road for his trips which would contribute to the minimization of aggregate travel costs. Aggregate travel costs would not be reduced by using some of the tolls collected from users of one road to support improvements on the other.

It should be noted that these felicitous interrelationships hold only when the two roads are in the equivalent of long run equilibrium. If either of the two roads has a capacity other than that which would minimize the total costs of trips between Here and There, it would not, in general, be desirable to equate the toll revenue generated by each road with its capital costs.

Expressway and street capacity in the typical urban area provides a real-world counterpart to the fast road in this example, while mass transport capacity is a counterpart of the slow road. There is evidence suggesting that expressway and street capacity is substantially less than that required to minimize total travel costs,[h] while excess mass transit capacity may well exist. If so, a toll system that would minimize the total cost of any given number of trips on a typical urban area's present transportation network could well involve the equivalent of bribes by private passenger vehicle operators to the users of mass transit systems. That is, under such conditions, minimizing total costs could require tolls on private passenger vehicles more than sufficient to cover the costs of streets and highways and mass transit fares that fall short of the cost of operating the mass transit system.

To suggest the orders of magnitude that might be involved, suppose that the capacity of the slow road between Here and There is equal to 1,118 vehicles per hour, about double the cost minimizing value given above, but that the fast road's capacity equals 950 vehicles per hour, only half of its optimum value. By trial and error methods, it can be found that minimizing the total time costs of trips would require 627 drivers to use the slow road and 1,000 − 627 = 373 to travel on the fast road. Inserting 627 for N, 6.27 cents for V, and 1,118 for K in equation (4-5) yields a marginal cost toll for the slow road of 2.649 cents per mile. Similar substitutions for the fast road yield a toll of 4.104 cents per mile. Substitution of $N = 627$ and $K = 1,118$ in equation (4-3) yields a travel time per mile on the slow road of 1.337 minutes. Similarly, travel time per mile on the fast road is 1.221 minutes. With these toll and time

---

[h]I have estimated that the travel time and vehicle operating cost savings that would result from new expressway capacity in the Minneapolis–St. Paul metropolitan area would involve rates of return on invested capital as high as 300 percent. Investment in expressways sufficient to increase their capacity to that of the present surface street network—a level of investment far beyond that presently contemplated—would still involve rates of return on the last unit of capacity installed of 35–60 percent. (See Mohring [2].)

combinations, the price of saving a minute by using the fast road is $(T_f - T_s)/(t_s - t_f)$ = 12.56 cents per mile. This value is just slightly in excess of that which driver 627, the slow road user with the highest travel time value, places on his time. Thus, just as when both roads are of optimum size, charging a marginal cost toll for each road would not just result in each driver's taking into account the cost his trips impose on others. It would also induce each driver to choose for his trips that road which would contribute to minimization of total travel costs.

Unlike the case in which both roads are of optimum size, marginal cost pricing under these circumstances would not result in each road's being self-supporting. If 627 drivers per hour use the slow road and each pays 2.649 cents per mile, it would generate total toll revenues of $16.60 per hour—149 percent of its hourly costs. The fast road would generate revenues of 373 travelers per hour times 4.104 cents per mile or $15.34 an hour—162 percent of its total cost.

One final implication of the analysis of these simple examples is worth noting. Going from a single optimum road to two roads of optimum size does result in a saving in the total costs of traveling between Here and There. Similarly, going from two optimum roads to two roads of nonoptimum size increases total travel costs. However, the cost differences among the three alternatives are surprisingly small. With a volume of 1,000 trips per hour and a capacity of 2,536 units, travel time per mile on a single road of optimum size turns out to be 1.222 minutes. Since the average value of a minute's time on the road is ten cents, total travel time costs per hour are $122.20 per mile. The hourly cost of 2,536 units of capacity is $25.36 per mile. Hence, total hourly costs on this road are $147.56 per mile.

With two roads of optimum size, the hourly cost of road capacity is $5.61 per mile for the slow road and $18.99 per mile for the fast road. The travel time cost to the 341 travelers per hour who use the slow road is $15.91 per mile, while for the 659 fast road users it is $105.40. The sum of these four cost components is $145.91—barely 1.5 percent less than the total cost for the single optimum road. Similarly, with the nonoptimum two-roads case, hourly capital costs on the two roads are $20.68 per mile while travel time costs are $126.65 per mile. Thus total hourly costs for this nonoptimum system are $147.33 per mile—less than 1 percent greater than the costs of the optimum two-road system.

The results of analyzing these very simple road networks provides what is at best a weak basis for generalization. Still, this analysis can be put into a broader context. Individual tastes in various commodities—furniture, clothing, housing, and automobiles, for example—do differ. This being the case, if no cost penalty is involved, society as a whole would seem better off if a variety of choices is available in these product groups than if alternatives are few in number. The more alternatives available, the more likely it is that each consumer will be able to find a combination of specifications that conforms closely to his tastes. So too with transportation routes. Tastes do differ. Most important, the rates at which individuals would be willing to exchange dollars for time do vary considerably. Thus, again if no cost penalty is involved, the availability of routes possessing a wide variety of toll and time combinations would clearly give each traveler a better chance of finding a personally optimum mode than if no choice was available. However, the fact that tastes differ does not in itself justify subsidizing either a particular product or those who buy it.

Appendix to Chapter Four

The Role of the Value of Travel Time in the Optimization and Pricing of Transportation Services

Considering a hypothetical bus line between Here and There is perhaps the simplest way to show how the disutility travelers incur from spending time in transit should be taken into account in optimizing and pricing transportation facilities.[i] Suppose that n consumers utilize the services of this bus line. Consumer i ($i = 1, \ldots, n$) derives utility from consuming a^i units per week of a general purpose commodity, dollars. He also derives utility from what happens There during each of the b^i trips per week he takes from Here to There and back. However, he incurs *disutility* from the time, $\tau^i = b^i t$, he spends traveling where t is the number of hours required to take a trip. Travel time per trip is a function, $t(B, X)$, of the total number of trips taken, $B = \Sigma b^i$, and of X, the total number of bus hours of service provided on the route each week.[j]

---

[i]This development leans heavily on the first of Strotz's "Urban Transportation Parables" [3].

[j]Implicit in this formulation is the assumption that the cost of a bus hour is independent of both the carrying capacity of the bus and the speed at which it travels. While clearly unrealistic, this assumption is not as bad as may at first seem to be the case. An increase in the capacity of a bus results in a less than proportionate increase in its capital, fuel, and related costs. More important, driver wages and fringe benefits account for about 70 percent of the total costs of a typical urban bus operation. The cost of a driver hour is independent of the size of the bus he operates.

This implicit assumption has two consequences for the analysis. First, there is always room aboard a bus for an additional passenger. That is, no one must ever wait for another bus to come because the first bus passing his stop is loaded to its capacity. Second, the bus company incurs no direct cost as the result of serving an additional passenger. The additional passenger affects the system only by increasing the travel time costs incurred by other passengers. Modifying the analysis to allow for bus capacity constraints and costs imposed on the bus company by additional passengers would not alter the conclusions reached in any fundamental sense.

Consumer i's problem, then, is to maximize his utility, $u^i(a^i, b^i, \tau^i)$ subject to his budget constraint, $I = a^i + Fb^i$ where F is the fare per bus round trip. Setting up the Lagrangian expression

$$z^i = u^i(a^i, b^i, \tau^i) + \lambda^i(I^i - a^i - Fb^i)$$

and differentiating with respect to a^i and b^i yields

$$z_a^i = u_a^i - \lambda^i = 0 \tag{4-7}$$

$$z_b^i = u_b^i + u_T^i\, t + u_T^i\, b\, t_B - \lambda^i F = 0 \tag{4-8}$$

as first order conditions for utility maximization where subscripts refer to partial derivatives. It seems reasonable to suppose that consumer i does not take into account the effect his trips have on his own travel time. If so, $u_T^i\, b\, t_B$ can be ignored. Amending equation (4-8) to take this assumption into account and dividing by equation (4-7) would then yield

$$u_b^i/u_a^i + t\, u_T^i/u_a^i = F \tag{4-9}$$

In equation (4-9), u_T^i/u_a^i, the ratio of the marginal disutility of travel time to the marginal utility of dollars has the dimension dollars per hour. It therefore seems reasonable to substitute for this ratio $-V^i$, the money cost consumer i attaches to his travel time. Doing so changes equation (4-9) to

$$u_b^i/u_a^i = u_b^i/\lambda^i = F + V^i t \tag{4-10}$$

This relationship says that consumer i will equate the ratio of the marginal utility of bus trips to that of dollars with the fare plus the time cost of a trip.

Suppose a public-spirited bus authority wishes to maximize a function, $W(u^1, \ldots, u^n)$, of the utility functions of bus users. In doing so, it is subject to the constraint $R = A + CX$ where R is the weekly flow of services available from the stock of resources at society's disposal. A is weekly consumption of dollars, Σa^i, and C is the number of units of resource services required to provide the services of a bus hour. Setting up the Lagrangian expression

$$Z = W(u^1, \ldots, u^n) + \eta(R - A - CX) \tag{4-11}$$

and differentiating with respect to a^i and b^i yields:

$$W_i u_a^i - \eta = W_i \lambda^i - \eta = 0 \tag{4-12}$$

$$W_i(u_b^i + u_T^i\, t) + \Sigma W_j u_T^j b^j\, t_B = 0 \qquad (4\text{-}13)$$

as first order conditions where W_i is $\partial W/\partial u^i$, the "marginal welfare weight" attached to individual i. The second equality in (4-12) follows from equation (4-7)—that is, it follows from the fact that consumer i will adjust his consumption of dollars so that their marginal utility equals his marginal utility of income, λ^i.

The authority responsible for providing bus service must take into account the fact that consumers will act so as to maximize their utility levels subject to the budget constraints with which they are faced. This fact permits substitution of equations (4-9), (4-10), and (4-12) into equation (4-13). On doing so, equation (4-13) can be shown to reduce to

$$\eta(F - BVt_B) = 0 \qquad (4\text{-}14)$$

where V equals the weighted (by number of trips taken) average value of an hour of travel time, $\Sigma b^i V^i/\Sigma b^i$. The Lagrangian multiplier, η, can be interpreted as the welfare gain resulting from a one unit increase in available resource services. It is presumably positive. If travel time is valued at V dollars an hour, the total weekly time cost of trips would be $T = BVt(B,X)$. Differentiating T with respect to B would yield an expression for the marginal time cost of a trip

$$\partial T/\partial B = Vt + BVt_B \qquad (4\text{-}15)$$

where, to repeat, subscripts refer to partial derivatives. The first term on the right of equation (4-15) can be interpreted as the average time cost of a trip. Hence BVt_B is the difference between average and marginal time costs—the costs an additional trip imposes on all other trip takers by increasing travel time per trip. Equation (4-14) can therefore be interpreted as saying that, if welfare is to be maximized, the fare per trip must equal the difference between the marginal and the average time costs of a trip; that is, the fare must equal the additional time costs resulting from an additional trip less those time costs incurred by the trip taker himself.

Differentiating equation (4-11) with respect to X, the number of bus hours of service provided, and making substitutions similar to those which led from equation (4-13) to equation (4-14) yield

$$- \eta(VBt_x + C) = 0 \qquad (4\text{-}16)$$

This is the same result that would follow from selecting the value of X that would minimize $VBt(B, X) + CX$, the total time and dollar costs of B trips if travel time is valued at V dollars an hour.

Chapter Five

The Value of Travel Time

The beginning of Chapter four raised an important question: What dollar values can reasonably be attached to various types of travel time? Unfortunately, the best available answer appears to be that no one really knows. Substantial problems arise in measuring the market value of most of those travel time inputs that are supplied by the consumers of transportation services. Few of these problems have been solved.

To elaborate, for reasons suggested by the discussion of efficient resource allocation in Chapter Two, the competitively determined market price of a commodity is a quite reasonable value to use in estimating the marginal benefits that would be derived from an expansion in its output. Similarly, the marginal social cost of a commodity can quite reasonably be regarded as the sum of the competitively determined market values of the inputs used in its production. Such valuation procedures can be applied with a fair degree of ease in dealing with inputs that are engaged entirely on the producing side of transportation activities—the time, for example, of truck, bus, and taxi drivers, airline pilots, railroad engineers and conductors, the conveyances they operate, the rights of way over which they travel, and the terminals at which they stop. Thus, the wage rates at which the services of pilots and stewardesses are purchased and the prices of the various other inputs required to provide an hour of airplane time can be determined, in principle, by carefully questioning those who participate in the markets in which these commodities are traded. Together, these price data provide a logical basis for determining *part* of the costs an additional airport landing would impose by delaying other flights, and hence a logical basis for determining *part* of an optimum set of airport user charges.

Similarly, information could be obtained in a quite straightforward, albeit costly, fashion on the wage rates of truck drivers, the prices of fuel and vehicle maintenance, the costs of trucks, the interest rates appropriate for valuing investments in them, and the effects of changes in highway characteristics and congestion levels on the rates at which these inputs are used. Such data would provide a direct basis for estimating *part* of the benefits that would derive from building additional highway capacity or otherwise improving an existing road network.

"Part" was italicized in the preceding paragraphs for good reason. There is at least one time input which is not directly involved in a market transaction in each of the examples discussed: the time of those who take airline trips in the former case; the time of commodities being transported in the latter. As for airlines, one might argue that passenger time ought to be valued in the same way as seems reasonable for pilot and stewardess time—at the wage rates commanded by passengers. After all, many—perhaps most—airline passengers travel on business. Furthermore, it can be argued that it is just as appropriate to use wage data in valuing leisure travel (or other leisure activities) as in valuing business travel. By engaging in leisure activities, an individual indicates a preference for the pleasures they provide over the pleasures derivable from purchasing additional market goods with the proceeds of additional hours spent at work.[a]

However, using earning rates to value passenger time requires an assumption that is not necessary in using earnings rates to value pilot and stewardess time—the assumption being that the average airline traveler would be indifferent between an additional hour spent aboard a plane and an additional hour spent at work. More generally, the use of earnings rates to value consumer-supplied travel time inputs in any form of passenger transportation—air, rail, automobile, bus, taxi—would be reasonable only if it could be assumed that the average traveler is indifferent between work and travel hours. The validity of such an assumption is clearly open to question.

Turning to the truck example, most shippers would likely prefer faster to slower transit times. At the very least, faster deliveries reduce the interest costs of holding inventories. In addition, shorter delivery times reduce the obsolescence costs of perishable commodities—many foodstuffs, newspapers, and high fashion clothing, for example. Then too, substantial random elements enter into the demands for many commodities. Examples include repair parts and goods such as air conditioners, fuel, and clothing for which demand is affected by weather conditions. For such commodities, lower delivery times can reduce or even eliminate the need for inventories at various stages of the production and distribution process.

[a]Ignored in this line of reasoning are the distortions introduced by the fact that the length of an individual's work week is typically more or less rigidly specified. This being the case, the representative worker is able only by accident to equate the marginal utility of leisure with the difference between the marginal disutility of work and the marinal utility of the consumption made possible by additional working hours. While this difficulty is clearly of relevance in discussing the applicability of wage rate data to the valuation of leisure travel, it is equally relevant to the use of wage rates in valuing any other human activity including work itself.

While most shippers prefer (and are willing to pay for) faster transit times, it is worth noting that many shippers would be willing to pay for *slower* transit times during some seasons. For example, cost considerations dictate that petroleum refineries and lumber and plywood mills operate at fairly constant output levels. The demands for petroleum refinery products, particularly fuel oils, have substantial winter peaks, while the demands for lumber and plywood have substantial summer peaks. Similarly, while the demand for canned foods exhibits little seasonal variation, canneries operate only at harvest times. For each of these and many other commodity groups, discrepancies between production and demand cycles result in substantial seasonal variations in finished goods inventories, and hence in substantial outlays for storage facilities. Storage requirements are particularly large immediately before seasonal demand peaks and immediately after seasonal production peaks. For the producers of such commodities, increases in off-peak delivery times correspondingly reduce the amounts and hence the costs of the storage space that they must provide themselves. Hence, they would be willing to pay at least limited premiums for slower delivery times.

To summarize: Of the various components of the value of time for goods in transit, only the interest costs of holding inventories can readily be determined with reasonable accuracy. For most commodities, this cost is a minor one. As for the values of human travel time, they are probably related to earnings rates—perhaps very closely. Fairly accurate earnings data can be obtained for those who travel by various modes. However, traveler time is a major transportation input. The difference between in transit and work activities is great. For these reason, the consequences and the likelihood of error seem substantial if earnings rates and travel time values are assumed to be equal. Attempts to determine travel time values by direct analysis of the many markets in which travel time is bought and sold in one way or another would therefore seem highly desirable.

Direct observations can be made of a number of market responses in which the value of travel time plays an important role. As far as I know, no systematic studies have been undertaken of responses involving the value to shippers of time in transit. Considerable work has been done, however, on the value of human time in transit.[b] Regretably, this research has led to conflicting results. Still, describing some of these studies will serve a useful purpose. The results are themselves of interest. In addition, they illustrate how, with a modicum of ingenuity, useful information can be extracted from unlikely places

[b]Much of this work is summarized in Stanford Research Institute [11] (Vol. I, ch. II).

and also, unfortunately, the pitfalls sometimes involved in the extraction process.

THE CHOICE OF SPEED MARKET

Consider first the simplest but perhaps least obvious of the markets in which travel time is traded. In the process of choosing the speed at which he travels, a driver is, in effect, trading time for money. An increase in realized speed clearly reduces the time required for a trip. At the same time, however, an increase in speed (at least above 30 miles an hour or so) definitely increases vehicle operating costs, probably increases accident costs,[c] and may affect both the probability that a driver will be convicted of a traffic violation and such pleasure or psychic stress as driving may provide. On a lightly traveled road a driver can attain his desired speed. Denote by $F(S)$ the nontime costs per mile of traveling at this speed, S miles per hour. Increasing S by one mile per hour would increase these nontime costs by $F(S + 1) - F(S)$ dollars. Evidence[d] suggests that $F(S + 1) - F(S)$ is an increasing function of s. At the same time, a one mile per hour increase in travel speed would reduce the time required to travel a mile by $1/S - 1/(S + 1)$ hours. This travel time reduction decreases with increases in S. For example, an increase from 29 to 30 miles per hour decreases travel time per mile by $60/29 - 60/30 = 0.069$ minutes. However, a speed increase from 59 to 60 miles per hour reduces time per mile by only $60/59 - 60/60 = 0.017$ minutes.

The increase in the nontime cost of travel divided by the time saving resulting from a speed increase—$[F(S + 1) - F(S)]/[1/S - 1/(S + 1)]$— can be interpreted as the price of saving travel time by increasing vehicle speed. To work with an admittedly unrealistic premise, suppose that accident costs are unrelated to travel speed and that drivers derive neither utility nor disutility from the act of driving fast. If so, the only costs incorporated in $F(S)$ are those of vehicle operation. Winfrey ([9], Appendix A) has developed data on the relationship between speed and operating costs for a 4,000-pound, 187-horsepower, late model automobile traveling on a straight, level, uncongested road. His data indicate that the price of saving time by increasing speed from 35 to 36 mph is 9 cents per hour. From 44-45 mph, the price is 40 cents per hour; from 55-56 mph, it is 78 cents per hour; and from 64-65, 74-75, and 79-80 mph respectively, it is $2.82, $6.11, and $10.27 per hour.

[c]It seems plausible to suppose that, if an accident occurs, its severity is approximately proportional to the square of the speed at which impact occurs. The probability that an accident will occur to a given vehicle is lowest when it travels at the average speed of the remaining vehicles on the road. This probability increases with increases (either positive or negative) in the difference between the speed of the given vehicle and that of the remaining vehicles.

[d]See, for example, the charts showing gasoline consumption at alternative speeds that appear in the operator's manuals for most automobiles.

The total cost of traveling a mile can be written

$$C = F(S) + V/S \qquad (5\text{-}1)$$

where V is the aggregate value the occupants of a vehicle attach to their time. It seems reasonable to suppose that travelers desire to minimize this total cost. If the speed at which they travel is such that the price they pay to save time is, say, less than the value they attach to it, they would lower their total costs by going faster. Trip costs would be minimized only at that speed for which[e]

$$[F(S + 1) - F(S)]/[1/S - 1/(S + 1)] = V \qquad (5\text{-}2)$$

i.e., at that speed for which the price of saving time equals the value attached to it.

Suppose again that (1) only time and vehicle operating costs vary with trip speed, (2) driving fast yields neither pleasure nor psychic stress, and in addition, (3) travelers are aware of the cost implications of alternative speeds and strive to minimize these costs. Under these circumstances, knowledge of an individual driver's $F(S)$ and his speed would suffice to determine the value he attaches to travel time. If, in addition to (1), (2), and (3), the Winfrey data are reasonably representative of all private passenger vehicles, knowledge of the distribution of speeds at which drivers would choose to travel on uncongested roads would suffice to determine any attribute of the distribution of travel time values that happens to be of interest.

Unfortunately, recent data on the distribution of desired speeds are unavailable. However, data presented by the U. S. Bureau of Public Roads [12] suggest that around 1950, desired speeds on high quality, straight, level rural highways were approximately normally distributed with a mean and standard deviation respectively of 48.5 and 8 miles per hour.[f] The AASHO "Red Book" (pp. 100-126) contains data from about the same time period on the relationship between desired speed on the one hand and tire wear and gasoline and oil consumption on the other. Using these data in the manner described above to develop prices of saving time at alternative speeds, multiplying the fraction of all drivers choosing to travel at each speed by the price at that speed, and summing over all travelers yields approximately $3.00 as the average cost of saving time for all travelers.

---

[e]A simpler relationship can be found by differentiating equation (5-1) and setting the result equal to zero: $V = S^2 \, dF(S)/dS$.

[f]With this distribution, approximately 14 percent of all travelers would choose speeds of less than 40 mph, 43 percent would travel at between 40-50 mph, 35 percent at between 50-60 mph, and the remaining 8 percent at speeds greater than 60 mph. (See U.S. Bureau of Public Roads [12], p. 32.)

THE CHOICE OF LOCATION MARKET

Residential real estate is another market in which travel time plays an important role. Other things being equal, most households probably prefer being close to the destinations of frequent trips—e.g., places of employment; schools; shopping, recreational, and cultural centers—and, indeed, would be willing to pay for such proximity. In a simply structured community, the value of proximity could be determined in a straightforward fashion from the spatial distribution of land values.

To be more specific, consider a hypothetical community located on an undifferentiated plain. In it, all commercial, industrial, recreational, and cultural activities take place at a single point: downtown. All families live in single family dwellings located on lots of the same size; all place the same value on their travel time; and all take the same number of trips downtown per month. The time required for a trip downtown is its only cost and is proportional to the crow-line distance between home and downtown. Given a choice between two lots at the same price, a family would choose the one with the smaller travel time. Indeed, the residential land market would be in equilibrium (a state in which no family would desire to move) only if the prices or rents for any two lots differ by an amount just sufficient to offset the difference between them in the cost of traveling downtown. If each family takes N round trips downtown a month, and if t_1 and t_2 are the times required to make round .trips from lots one and two, then the difference between the monthly rents on these two lots would be

$$R_1 - R_2 = NV(t_2 - t_1) \qquad (5\text{-}3)$$

where R refers to rent and V is the value of travel time.

Quite similar conclusions would hold for more realistically structured communities. Continue, for simplicity, to suppose that only one destination, downtown, is of relevance to a household, and that the area surrounding downtown is an undifferentiated plain. However, let the number of trips a household takes depends on both their time and their money costs. Similarly, let the size of the lot on which the household builds its house depend on the price of land. As with the simpler city, the price of land would decrease with distance from downtown. It can be shown (see Mohring [7]) that a household in such a city would maximize the utility it derives from its (by assumption) fixed income if it locates at that destination from downtown for which

$$2N(V + dC/dt) = L(dR/dt) \qquad (5\text{-}4)$$

In this expression, N is the number of round trips taken downtown per month (a function of the time and money cost of trips and perhaps other prices as well), V is the value of travel time, and dC/dt is the rate at which the money cost of a one-way trip increases with increases in travel time per trip. L is the size of the lot on which the household chooses to live (a function of the price of land and perhaps other prices as well), and dR/dt is the rate at which the rent per acre of residential land decreases with increases in the time required for a trip downtown. Equation (5-4) says, then, that the household will maximize its utility by locating so that moving a bit further from downtown would result in an increase in the time and money costs of travel that would be exactly offset by a reduction in the cost of its housing site.

At least two attempts have been made to estimate travel time values by using the analytical framework underlying equation (5-3) while a third has been based on a more refined version of the analysis leading to equation (5-4). In the first of these studies (Mohring [6]), I concluded that the relationship between travel time to downtown Seattle and the prices involved in postwar sales of vacant suburban residential lots implied an average travel time value of $0.50-$1.00 per hour for an individual traveler.

In the second of these studies, Pendleton [8] pointed out that I had not adjusted my results to reflect the increased vehicle operating costs associated with increased travel times. He found a relationship between travel time to downtown Washington D.C. and the prices of otherwise comparable dwelling units in 1961 that was almost identical to mine for Seattle. However, on adjusting this relationship to reflect differences in vehicle operating costs, he concluded, "it is clear that the estimated value of 1.26 cents per minute does not even cover the saving in operating costs and implies a zero or negative valuation of travel time" ([8], p. 53).

In a third study, which analyzed residential real estate prices in Minneapolis and the travel patterns of University of Minnesota faculty members, Maslove [5] dropped the restrictive assumptions that tastes are uniform and that travel rates and lot sizes are independent of location. He also generalized equation (5-5) to take into account the fact that destinations other than downtown are of importance to households, and that the values of residences are affected by features of their immediate environment such as proximity to parks or railroad tracks and the values of neighboring houses. Maslove's findings were, if anything, even less felicitous than those of Pendleton's and my studies. He found site values to be negatively related only to distance from the nearest major regional shopping center. Site values appeared to *increase* with distance from the two centers that generate the greatest numbers of trips in the city—the Minneapolis central business district and the University of Minnesota campus.

THE ROUTE AND MODE CHOICE MARKETS

A third type of market in which travel time can be exchanged for money arises when trips between pairs of points can be made by alternative routes or travel modes that differ in the time and money outlays required. The "two roads" optimization problem discussed in Chapter Four is a hypothetical example of such a market. Several attempts have been made to infer the values travelers attach to their time through the analysis of consumer behavior in real-world counterparts of this market.

In what is among both the simplest and the best of these studies, Beesley [1] analyzed the commuting patterns of a group of civil servants working for the Ministry of Transport in London.[g] Of the 1,450 employees who responded to his questionnaire, 1,109 gave complete information and also indicated that they had alternative ways of traveling to work. For some, the choice was between two mass transit routes; for the remainder, the choice was between automobile on the one hand and a single mass transit route on the other. The preferred route of two-thirds of these respondents involved both greater speed and a lower money cost. However, 27.5 percent of the respondents (Beesley referred to them as "traders") were faced with situations in which the preferred route was either faster but more expensive or slower but cheaper than its alternative.

As was suggested in Chapter Four, the difference for traders between the money costs of travel along the two routes, divided by the difference between their respective travel times, can be regarded as the price of saving time by taking the faster route. A trader who chooses his faster alternative reveals by this choice that he values travel time at more than the price he must pay to save it. Similarly, a trader who chooses his slow alternative indicates his travel time value to be less than the price of saving it. To put it differently, information on the choice of a single trader yields an upper or a lower bound to the value he attaches to travel time, but not, unfortunately, an exact value.

However, if a group of people could be found who are identical in all but the prices they face for saving travel time, their collective value of the time could reasonably be argued to be that price above which all (or most) group members choose the slow route and below which all (or most) choose the fast route. Beesley's criterion of similarity was, logically enough, civil service grade and hence, within a small range, annual salary. Only two salary groups of traders who chose between alternative mass transit routes were sufficiently numerous to support detailed analysis: Clerical Officers, whose annual salaries averaged $1,820 at the exchange rate and price levels current in the mid 1960s, and Executive Officers with an average annual salary of $2,380. He found that for Clerical Officers and Executive Officers, respectively, travel time values equivalent at the time to 28 and 45 cents an hour minimized the number of "misclassifications." A "misclassified" traveler was one who either chose the fast

---

[g]The description that follows differs in some respects from that of Beesley's article [1]. Changes were made to conform more closely to preceding portions of this chapter. They hopefully do no appreciable violence to his analysis.

route at a price higher than the time value assigned to his group, or who chose the slow route at a price lower than this time value.[h]

Commuting in an automobile and in a mass transit conveyance are different experiences. One provides privacy and a guaranteed seat but requires coping with rush hour traffic. The other avoids this latter unpleasantness but typically involves crowding, noise, and dirt. For a representative traveler, the unpleasantness incurred per minute of travel may well differ for mass transit and automobile trips. In Beesley's study, the numbers determined through analysis of choices between alternative mass transit routes were, in effect, accepted as *the* values of travel time. These values, together with information from those travelers who chose between automobile and mass transit trips, were then used to infer the differential unpleasantness (call it D_a) of a minute spent traveling in an automobile.

Let V refer to the value of (mass transit) travel time, t_a and t_b be the respective times required for automobile and bus trips, and C_a and C_b be their respective money costs. The price of a bus trip can be regarded as the sum of its time and money costs, $Vt_b + C_b$. Similarly, the price of an automobile trip is the sum of its time, differential unpleasantness, and money costs $(V + D_a)t_a + C_a$. If a commuter chooses to travel by automobile, he reveals that for him the former price is greater than the latter—i.e., that

$$Vt_b + C_b > (V + D_a)t_a + C_a$$

On rearranging terms, this relationship can be seen to imply that

$$[V(t_b - t_a) + C_b - C_a]/t_a > D_a$$

[h]The procedure Beesley [1] followed can most easily be visualized by conceiving of a table with three columns. The first shows, in ascending order, the price of saving time faced by each member of the group being studied. The second and third are respectively headed, "revealed travel time value greater than," and "revealed travel time value less than." If, for example, three people take the fast route at a price of 2 cents a minute, the number "3" would be entered in the 2-cents-per-minute row of the second column. Similarly, if four people take the slower route at a price of 7 cents per minute, a "4" would be entered in the 7-cent row of the third column. One would expect most entries in this table to be either toward the top of the second column or toward the bottom of the third column, with entries occurring in both columns only toward the middle of the table. The "minimum misclassification travel time value" could then be found by proceeding down this table to (one of) the point(s) where a movement one line further down would result in a reduction in the number of misclassified column two entries that would just be offset by an increase in the number of column three misclassifications.

Fairly large fractions—27 percent of the clerical officers and 25 percent of the executive officers—were "misclassified" in this sense. In addition to differences in travel time values within civil service classes, Beesley recognized that this phenomenon resulted at least partially from the fact that he failed to differentiate among types of travel time in his analysis. As will be developed later, there is considerable evidence that travelers would pay more to save a minute spent walking to mass transit stops or waiting there for service to come than to save a minute aboard a mass transit conveyance.

Similarly, choice of a mass transit trip implies the left-hand side of this relationship to be less than D_a.

In Beesley's analysis, the value of D_a that minimized misclassifications turned out to be zero for Clerical Officers. For Executive Officers a D_a value of 7 cents did so—that is, automobile travel appeared to be 7 cents an hour more unpleasant than mass transit travel for these civil servants. Limited experimentation with a small group of respondents with salaries in excess of $6,200 a year yielded estimates of mass transit travel time values in the $1.40–$1.75 an hour range and values of D_a amounting to about 5 percent of these figures.

An important reservation is in order regarding the values assigned to D_a. Critical in their estimation were the numbers used to specify automobile operating costs. Beesley assumed that the out-of-pocket expenses of vehicle operation are the only costs considered in deciding whether to use mass transit or a private passenger vehicle in the journey to work. This is a very common assumption. However, as will be developed at greater length later in the concluding section of this chapter, there is good reason to suppose that out-of-pocket expenses understate the true costs of relevance. To the degree that they do, Beesley recognized that his figures overstate the differential unpleasantness of commuting by automobile.

Of perhaps greater interest than the specific money values of travel time Beesley obtained is the relationship between these values and the income levels with which they were associated. For the lowest salary group, the Clerical Officers, the value of both mass transit and automobile travel time was about 31 percent of the group's average wage rate. For Executive Officers, the fraction was 36 percent for mass transit travel and 42 percent for automobile travel. Finally, for the highest paid group, the fraction appeared to fall between 42–52 percent for mass transit and 45–55 percent for automobile.

In a situation similar to that studied by Beesley, Lisco [4] obtained comparable results through use of a considerably more laborate statistical technique, multiple probit analysis. The specific situation with which he dealt was the choice between public transportation and private passenger vehicle by commuters to the Loop (the central portion of Chicago's central business district) from a northern suburb, Skokie, which had recently been provided with a subway link. Without going into the details of his estimating procedure, it can roughly be interpreted as determining the probability that an individual with specified attributes (income, age, alternative travel costs by the two modes, etc.) will choose subway rather than automobile for his trips to work.

Consider two individuals whose characteristics are identical except that the first must spend 5 minutes more than the second if he travels by subway, but pay 25 cents more if he travels by auto. Suppose also that the probability of using the subway is the same for both. This means that a 25 cent increase in price and a 5 minute increase in travel time have the same effect on the probability of taking a trip by subway. These travelers therefore act as if time has a value to them of 5 cents a minute or $3.00 an hour.

As did Beesley, Lisco attempted to distinguish between what can be termed a pure travel time value and a comfort and convenience value.[i] As for the former, in those income groups in which a reasonably large number of respondents was found, the ratio of travel time value to income increased from about 25 percent for those with $6,000 incomes to 50 percent for those with $10,000 incomes. Above $10,000, the ratio remained approximately constant at 50 percent. Despite the unpleasantness of rush hour traffic, commuters appeared willing to pay for the privilege of traveling in their automobiles rather than in crowded, unattractive subway cars. These values ranged from 78 cents per trip for a $6,000 a year traveler to $2.53 for one with a $10,115 income, and $3.18 for one making $13,500 a year.

Just as spending time aboard a mass transit vehicle may be more or less pleasant than spending time driving a car to work, the pleasantness of the various activities that enter into traveling by one mode or another may differ. Thus a representative traveler may regard the walk from his home to a mass transit station or from a parking lot to his office as being more or less pleasant than being aboard a subway car or driving an automobile. Although both Beesley and Lisco recognized that consumers may place different time values on the various activities which enter into travel activities, neither incorporated this possibility into their formal analyses. Lisco did, however, undertake a separate, limited study of the structure of parking lot rates in the area surrounding the Loop. Most people prefer short rather than long walks from parking lots to their ultimate destinations. Casual observation reveals that, presumably for this reason, parking lot rates decline fairly sharply with distance from the major employment and shopping concentrations in central business districts. Consider two parking lots, one a block closer to a central business district than the other. The difference in the parking rates for an 8-9-hour stay, divided by twice the time required to walk a block, is the price a commuter must pay to save walking time on the round-trip journey between his office and his parking lot.

In areas where commuters dominate parking lot use, market forces presumably lead to rate differentials for 8-to 9-hour stays that reflect the willingness of commuters to pay for the privilege of saving walking time—that is, the value of walking time can be inferred from the price of saving it. While rate differentials did differ somewhat among the streets Lisco studied, the patterns were all quite similar to that along Clark Street. There, the price for an all day stay declined linearly from approximately $3.00 to 75 cents in the space of just under half a mile. If a commuter's average walking speed is 3 miles per hour, this price differential works out to almost exactly twelve cents a minute or $7.20 an hour. For all the travelers in Lisco's multiple probit analysis study, the

---

[i]In Lisco's [4] analysis, the specific numbers attached to these two values depended on how the effect of income on the choice of travel mode was allocated between the pure travel time and the comfort and convenience components. The numbers cited here are those he regards as most likely. (See [4], pp. 53-56.)

pure travel time (as distinct from the comfort and convenience) component of trip costs averaged out to be almost exactly 4 cents a minute. Thus, the disutility of walking appears to be about three times that of riding for the average commuter. To put it differently, the discomfort of walking—independent of the time it occupies—is valued by the average Chicago commuter at 8 cents a minute.

Most route and mode choice analyses of the value of travel time have dealt with the journey to work decision. However, some studies have been undertaken in other travel markets. Among the best of these is Gronau's [3] study of long distance passenger transportation. Attention will be restricted here to that portion of his findings which is of relevance to travel by unaccompanied individuals.[j] An analysis of 1963 data on coach fares and the fastest scheduled times for trips by air (*a*), rail (*r*), and bus (*b*) between New York and the 38 most frequent travel destinations from that city led to the conclusion that both fares (*F*, measured in dollars) and travel time (*t*, measured in hours) are linearly related to distance (*D*, measured in miles):[k]

$$F_a = 7.04 + .0601\ D \tag{5-5a}$$
$$F_r = 5.59 + .0427\ D \tag{5-5b}$$
$$F_b = 3.56 + .0326\ D \tag{5-5c}$$

$$t_a = 2.56 + .0021\ D \tag{5-6a}$$
$$t_r = -0.59 + .0254\ D \tag{5-6b}$$
$$t_b = -0.32 + .0284\ D \tag{5-6c}$$

These relationships indicate that for trips of more than 135 miles, travelers had the sort of opportunity to trade time for money with which Beesley's study was concerned. Thus, for a 150-mile trip, travel time by air, rail, and bus were, respectively, 2.875, 3.223, and 3.942 hours, while the respective fares were $17.61, $13.10, and $9.30. Taking the difference between air and rail fares and dividing by the corresponding difference in travel times yields $(F_a - F_r)/(t_r - t_a) = (\$17.61 - \$13.10)/(3.223 - 2.875) = \$11.67$ as the price of saving an hour by using the faster mode. The corresponding calculation for the comparison between bus and rail yields $4.92 per travel hour. Thus, anyone valuing his travel time at more than $11.67 would have used air for a 150-

---

[j]According to Gronau's [3] data, auto trips are both slower and, for distances of more than 90 miles, more costly than bus trips for unaccompanied individuals. For longer distance trips, auto is dominated by other modes unless some combination of two or more individuals traveling together and the need for a car at destination are involved.

[k]The relationships for air include estimates of the time and money required to reach the airports involved. The bus and rail relationships ignore these costs.

mile trip. A travel time value of less than $5.92 would induce bus travel while those people with time values between $5.92 and $11.67 would use rail.

The price of saving time by air travel diminishes sharply with distance. Thus, for a 200-mile trip in 1963, what was referred to in Chapter Four as an individual's full price for an air trip would be lower than his full price for a bus trip[1] if he valued his travel time at more than $3.67 an hour. The corresponding figures for 500- and 2,500-mile trips are $1.67 and $1.15. As one might expect on the basis of this information, air's share of total passenger travel increases with trip distance. Gronau [3] collected data from the 1963 Census of Transportation indicating that air was used by 1, 8, and 23 percent of all travelers who made trips of, respectively, 100-199, 200-499, and 500 or more miles. Air's corresponding shares of trips made by common carrier were 20, 57, and 70 percent.

Gronau used this information, together with Census data on the income distribution of travelers, to draw crude inferences about the relationship between the value of travel time and hourly earnings. Suppose that travel time values are perfectly correlated with income—i.e., that the 70 percent of all common carrier travelers who used air were also the 70 percent with the highest incomes. In 1963, $4,700 was the approximate annual family income that divided the top 70 percent of all common carrier travelers from the bottom 30 percent. The 1960 Census of Population suggests $2.20 to have been about the average hourly earnings rate of a member of a family with a $4,700 income.

The prices of time implied by the air-bus choice are, as mentioned above, $1.67 for a 500-mile trip and $1.15 for a 2,500-mile trip. The average of these values if $1.41, or about 65 percent of the marginal traveler's hourly earnings rate. Similar calculations for the choice between auto and air travel for 200-500 mile trips led Gronau to a dividing line between air and auto traveler family incomes of about $14,400 and a value of time of $2.30—about 60 percent of the $3.90 average hourly earnings rate for such a family. Gronau regarded these calculations as providing only supporting evidence for his main conclusions about the value of travel time. These conclusions were based on an analysis of data provided by the Port of New York Authority on the characteristics of 13,822 air travelers between New York and the 38 destinations on which equations (5-5) and (5-6) are based. Without going into the full details of his regression analysis, it included the assumption that the full price of traveler *i*'s air trip (the sum of its dollar cost and his valuation of the time it

---

[1]For trips of 176 miles, an individual who valued his travel time at more than $4.73 would have chosen air over rail. At this distance, an individual with a travel time value of less than $4.76 would have chosen bus over rail. Thus, for trips of more than 175 miles, rail dropped out of contention for patrons. Anyone with a travel time value less than that sufficient to justify air travel would have gone by bus.

requires) can be written $P_i = F_a + k W_i t_a$. In this expression, W_i is traveler i's hourly earnings rate and k is a constant assumed to apply to travelers of all income levels.

Gronau's results differed somewhat from one specific form of estimating relationship to another and, more important, between business and personal travel. For business trips, the k value estimates ranged around one—that is, business travelers (or their employers) appear "to view traveling time as working time lost and, hence, assign to [travel] time a value that equals the foregone output" ([3], p. 4). Contrary to the implications of the introduction to this chapter, however, these findings did not carry over to personal travel. For personal air trips, Gronau found k values that were close to zero—that is, an air traveler's time value for a personal trip appeared to bear no close relationship to his earnings rate.

RECONCILING THE MARKET DATA

The results of these empirical studies are, unfortunately, inconsistent. The land value studies and Gronau's analysis of nonbusiness long distance travel suggest that people are either indiffent to the amount of time they spend traveling, or that they actually enjoy it and are deterred from doing more of it only by the money costs of their trips. The results of the choice of route and choice of speed studies are inconsistent in important respects. The $3.00 an hour average for all travelers from the choice of speed study is based on data from the early 1950s and on the conservative assumptions that neither accident costs nor the psychic stress of driving is related to speed. Lisco's analysis suggests $3.00 an hour to be about the value a $12,000 a year commuter would attach to his travel time in the mid 1960s. Twelve thousand dollars a year was hardly an average income in the early 1950s. When the difference between British and American money wage levels is taken into account, the relationships between income and the value of travel time found by Beesley and Lisco are gratifyingly similar. However, the studies do differ in that Beesley found traveling in an automobile to be more unpleasant than using mass transit, while Lisco found the reverse to be true. An attempt to reconcile these disparities seems in order.

The assumptions that must be satisfied if $3.00 an hour (or a comparable figure based on more recent data) is to be accepted as the average value of automobile travel time are restrictive—indeed, implausible. It seems unlikely that most drivers are aware of the precise relationship between the speed at which they travel and the costs of operating their vehicles. Other costs likely enter into the calculations of those few who are aware of this relationship. In particular, fear of accidents is likely to be a greater deterrent to higher speeds than the desire to avoid increased vehicle operating costs. On the other hand, for at least some drivers, speed is an end rather than a means in traveling. In brief, the cost implications of alternative travel speeds and the distribution of travelers' chosen speeds cannot be regarded as giving conclusive evidence regarding the value of travel time.

Taken by itself, proximity to major centers of economic activity is almost certainly a desirable locational attribute for most urban households. However, distance from major foci of economic activity in the central city of a typical urban area is almost certainly positively related to a number of attributes that most households find desirable: putatively better schools in outlying areas, proximity to open space, distance from central city ghetto dwellers. None of the three land value studies was able to take these factors into account.

Even if these factors are not important, conditions exist that make it unreasonable to suppose that the spatial equilibrium relationship, equation (5-4), holds for all or even possibly a substantial fraction of households. A considerable number of the University of Minnesota faculty members questioned by Maslove indicated that they were in states of spatial disequilibrium. That is, they would have preferred either lots of different sizes or locations at different distances from the central business district and the University of Minnesota campus than those they then owned or rented. They were presumably deterred from seeking more suitable locations by the high costs of doing so in terms not only of money but also of time and the disruption of established living patterns.

From the discussion of the real estate and choice of speed markets, it appears that if transactions in markets in which travel time plays an important role are to be used to infer the values travelers attach to it, these markets must possess at least two important characteristics. First, unlike the choice of speed market, those who trade in a market must be aware of the price they are paying for time; and second, unlike the real estate market, the cost of changing established purchasing patterns must be small.

Although trips of the sort studied by Gronau are taken infrequently, they are sufficiently high in cost that it seems reasonable to suppose that the travelers involved make themselves familiar with the options open to them. Similarly, both the Beesley and Lisco studies involved trips taken with sufficient frequency that those studied can reasonably be assumed to have accurate information about the consequences of alternative travel decisions. When account is taken of the differences between British and American price and salary structures, the results of these two studies appear remarkably similar. The only serious difference between them is their conflict over whether a comfort premium attaches to mass transit or to private passenger vehicles. Differences between the London and Chicago transportation systems cannot reasonably be held to account for this conflict. Coping with Chicago and London rush hour traffic is almost equally painful, and while the London underground might not win over the Chicago subway in a contest for filthiness, the race would be close.

Reconciliation of this conflict probably lies in one finding of Lisco's study that has not yet been mentioned. In estimating the discomfort component of automobile travel, Beesley made what is an almost universal assumption in this sort of work: The short run marginal costs of operating a vehicle are the only costs of relevance in trip taking decisions. This assumption is presumably based on the fact that the costs of automobile licenses, insurance, the capital invested in an automobile, that portion of depreciation on it which would occur independently of its use, and perhaps other annual outlays as well, are all sunk costs. Since they do not vary with use of the automobile, they can properly be ignored in deciding whether to make additional trips.

As far as it goes, this reasoning is perfectly sound. However, it overlooks an important ramification of the fact that automobiles are lumpy assets. Households cannot easily alter auto ownership as their demands for automobile services vary in the short run. Even though few automobile owners have use for their cars while sleeping, no markets exist in which auto services can be sold during those time periods. Similarly, there are rental markets in which a household can acquire automobile services in addition to those derivable from the car(s) it owns. However, prices in these markets are so high that travelers use them only under rather special circumstances.

If an unmarried worker lives alone, or if the spouse of a married worker is unable to drive, their automobiles (if they own them) would go unused if they are not driven to work. For these drivers, the out-of-pocket cost of automobile operation—gasoline, oil, tire wear, use related maintenance—is truly the only relevant cost in deciding whether to commute by auto or by mass transit. If the spouse of a married worker is able to drive, however, his use of their car to commute deprives her of its use in his absence. If he commutes by car, the relevant costs of his trip are not just those of vehicle operation but also the opportunity costs of the vehicle itself—in this case, the loss to her of whatever utility she would have derived from using the car had it been left at home. One step further: If the spouse of a married worker not only can drive, but actually must herself use a car to commute, then a decision by him to drive to work is effectively a decision to buy an additional car. For him, the cost relevant to this decision process is the *full* cost of a second car, not just that of operating it.

In his analysis, Lisco regarded the direct cost of automobile trips to be parking costs plus, alternatively, 6 or 9 cents a mile traveled. In addition, he segregated his respondents into three-family composition groups. An individual was included in the first group *if* he was unmarried *or* if his spouse either could not drive or drove to work with him. A commuter who had a working spouse who drove to work independently of him was included in the second group. The third group, all others, included mainly "normal" families—i.e., married commuters whose spouses had driving licenses but who did not commute to work by automobile themselves.

Membership in the first group produced results 38-40 cents[m] per round trip more favorable to automobile commutation than did membership in the third. That is, two otherwise identical members of the first and third group would have the same probability of taking the subway only if traveling by car cost the former 38-40 cents more than the latter. Similarly membership in the second group yielded results $2.10-$2.26 *less* favorable to automobile round trips. The opportunity costs of an automobile to an auto driving but noncommuting spouse (38-40 cents a day) implied by this analysis seem rather small. Further checking revealed that a large fraction of those in group one were unmarried individuals living with their parents.

> Apparently the number of single commuters who would not own their own cars regardless of commuting needs, is fairly large, and this counteracts the effect of commuters who are either married with a non-driving spouse, or who are unmarried and would own a car anyway ([4], p. 57).

It is of interest to relate to another set of data the $2.10-$2.26 opportunity cost implied for those in group two. The U.S. Bureau of Public Roads periodically develops automobile operating cost figures. Cope and Gauthier [2] made such computations in February 1970 for a four-door sedan with an initial cost of $3,374 and operated 100,000 miles over a ten-year period in Baltimore. Total costs (excluding foregone interest) under these assumptions were $11,890. Of this total, $2,059 reflected insurance and license fees—costs that are independent of the rate at which the vehicle is operated. Depreciation, maintenance, and repairs accounted for an additional $4,706. On the order of half these costs are also independent of the rate at which the vehicle is operated. Adding insurance and licensing costs to one-half of depreciation, maintenance, and repairs, and dividing this total by 5 days per week times 50 weeks per year times 10 years, yields $1.77—33-49 cents less than Lisco's numbers—as the approximate daily fixed cost (ignoring interest) of an automobile used primarily for commuting.

The value that Beesley imputed to the additional unpleasantness of automobile driving amounted to about 7 cents per hour of travel time for both Executive Officers and higher civil servants. Again, this imputation is based on the implicit assumption that all of their automobiles have zero opportunity costs. Had Beesley been able to add vehicle opportunity costs to direct operating costs in his analysis, it seems quite likely that he, too, would have found that a comfort premium attached to automobiles, and not to mass transit.

---

[m]The first number resulted when vehicle operating costs were assumed to be 6 cents a mile, the second for 9 cents a mile.

In conclusion, then, only the following assertions about the amounts travelers would be willing to pay to reduce travel time can presently be made with reasonable assurance. For commuters, these amounts appear closely related to their wage rates or the hourly equivalent of their annual salaries. Specifically, workers with incomes equivalent to about $5,000 a year at prices in effect during the mid 1960s appear willing to pay about 25–30 percent of their hourly wage rate to save travel time. Increases in income above that level are associated with increases in the ratio of travel time value to wage rate. Beyond $10,000–$12,000 a year (again in mid 1960s prices) this ratio appears to stabilize at about 50 percent. In making long distance air trips, businessmen appear to treat an hour spent traveling as an hour lost from other business activities. They therefore value business travel hours at about the equivalent wage of these other business activities. However, no evidence of a relationship between income and travel time values is apparent from the study of long distance trips made for nonbusiness purposes.

Chapter Six

The Peak Load and Related Cost Allocation Problems

Cost allocation is a problem to which little attention is paid in the general economics literature. In part, the reasons for this lack of attention are obvious. The typical discussion of business firm behavior assumes the firm to produce a single product. Demand for this product remains fixed over a substantial period of time. The cost allocation problem faced by such a firm is trivial, as each unit of output is produced under conditions identical to that for every other unit. Assigning the same average cost to all units is therefore the obvious thing to do. At the same time, however, cost allocation is typically not discussed even in dealing with the behavior of joint or multiproduct firms.[a] This neglect probably reflects the fact that, even for such a firm, marginal costs are the only ones of relevance in specifying the profit maximizing price and output level for each of its products. Maximizing profits does not require determining the "average cost" of any individual product.

Cost allocation is, however, a problem to which considerable attention is given in discussions of the economic problems of transportation and public utility firms. For example, the generating capacity required by an electric power company is determined by the annual peak demand for its services that typically occurs late in a weekday afternoon between December 15-25 or during the middle of a hot July afternoon. Not all buyers participate equally in this peak demand. This fact quite naturally leads to questions about how the so-called "common costs" of generating capacity should be allocated among customer classes. These questions are usually[b] couched in terms such as: Should a user who does not contribute to the system peak be allowed to pay only the variable costs of the power he consumes? Or, since he benefits from the ex-

[a]See, for example, the discussion of "joint products" in Henderson and Quandt [4], pp. 89-98.

[b]Garfield and Lovejoy [3], pp. 134-228, for example, contains an extended discussion of conventional approaches to answering these questions.

istence of generating capacity, should he be forced to bear a share of its costs even though his consumption in no way adds to these costs? If so, what is the equitable way of assessing some of these costs against him?

Most transportation systems also have serious peak load problems. To take an extreme example, during the afternoon commuter rush, traffic volumes on most urban highway networks are a hundred or more times their levels at 2-4 a.m. Another cost allocation problem involved in the provision of highway services has also received considerable attention. It arises out of the following sorts of considerations. If only because thinner pavements would be required, a highway designed exclusively to serve private passenger vehicles would be less costly to construct than one that includes heavy trucks among its users. Indeed, once a highway authority has decided on the heaviest axle load for which a highway should be designed, allowing the road to be used by lighter vehicles would involve negligible added pavement costs. This being the case, should taxes to cover pavement costs be levied only on the heaviest vehicles? Or should all vehicle owners share in these costs even though many vehicles have no effect on pavement thickness? If so, what is the equitable way of allocating costs among individual user classes?[c]

This chapter is devoted to these and related problems in allocating the joint or common or overhead costs of multiproduct activities to individual product classes. To state the conclusion at the outset: If (1) the price charged each customer class or during each time period is set equal to the short run marginal cost of providing the commodity, and (2) production involves constant returns to scale and is organized so as to minimize total costs, then (3) total revenues will exactly cover total costs—no overhead or joint or common costs will remain to be allocated. This conclusion applies, it should be emphasized, only to activities characterized by constant returns to scale. If an activity involves economies of scale, then marginal cost pricing coupled with cost minimization will generate revenues insufficient to cover total costs. The problem of having residual costs to be allocated arises because of increasing returns, however, not because of the joint nature of the production process.

MUTTON AND WOOL AND THE BACK-HAUL PROBLEM: COST ALLOCATION WITH FIXED PROPORTIONS

Two sorts of joint production processes are commonly distinguished in the economics literature. First are those processes in which commodities must be produced in rigidly fixed proportions—mutton and wool from a particular type of sheep,[d] as an example. Second, and far more common, are those processes in

---

[c]Various proposals for answering these questions for highways are developed in U.S. Bureau of Public Roads [10] (Part IV) and [11], and in Meyer et al. [6], pp. 65–85.

[d]Sheep that, it must additionally be assumed, can be slaughtered only on the birthday at which they cease being lambs. This additional assumption is required to eliminate the possibility of altering the wool-mutton output ratio by adjusting the number of wool crops obtained from one animal.

which the marginal cost of any one product is affected by the rates at which other products are produced. The output mix obtainable from a given type of crude oil processed in a given petroleum refinery provides an example. This mix typically is varied substantially from season to season. In summer, operating conditions are selected so as to yield relatively high gasoline outputs, albeit at relatively high marginal costs. In winter, operating conditions are selected to raise fuel oil output and the marginal cost of gasoline is relatively low. Joint products that are produced under variable proportions will be considered in the following sections of this chapter.

If wool and mutton are produced in fixed proportions, it is logically impossible to specify the cost of a pound of either, given only information on the cost of raising a sheep. At the same time, however, if the market price of wool is known, it is reasonable to regard the "marginal cost" of a sheep's worth of mutton as the cost of raising an additional sheep less the revenue that would be derived from the sale of its wool. Suppose the market price of mutton happens to equal its marginal cost, in this sense of the term. Suppose also that sheep raising involves constant returns to scale. That is, suppose that the cost of raising an additional sheep is independent of the number of sheep raised. Then the revenue derived from selling a sheep's worth of mutton and wool would just equal the cost of raising the sheep. No joint costs would remain to be allocated. If the price of mutton happens not to equal its marginal cost, then neither the mutton nor the wool markets is in equilibrium. If, for example, the marginal cost of mutton happens to be less than its price, sheep raisers would have a clear incentive to expand output. Doing so would increase the supplies of both mutton and wool. The market prices of both commodities would therefore tend to fall until, in equilibrium, the prices of both wool and mutton would equal their marginal costs.

This line of reasoning can be applied directly to the so-called "back-haul" problem experienced in most transportation activities. Clearly, an additional shipment from There to Here would cost less if an empty truck is already at There than if an empty vehicle must be sent for it from Here. Indeed, conversations with truckers suggest that, apart from the additional pickup, delivery, and terminal costs that may be involved, there is no appreciable difference between the costs of sending loaded and empty vehicles between any two points. While a loaded truck would consume more fuel (particularly on a hilly road), an empty truck would require more maintenance (particularly on a bumpy road).

Suppose that the cost of a truck round trip between Here and There is independent both of the rate at which trips are made and, except for loading costs, of whether one leg of the trip is made empty. Suppose also that a competitively organized trucking industry initially provides N truck round trips a week between these two points. Market forces could be expected to establish that price for Here-There truck trips at which shippers would buy N truck loads a week of transportation services and similarly for trips between There and

Here. In this initial equilibrium, the price for a Here-There trip plus that for a There-Here trip need not equal the cost of a truck round trip. If these two prices sum to more than this cost, existing or new truck companies would profit from supplying additional round trips. The prices of Here-There and There-Here shipments would both fall. Similarly, if the sum of the two prices is less than the cost of a round trip, trucks would be withdrawn from Here-There service, thereby increasing the price of trips in both directions. Regardless of the initial relationship between the cost and the prices of trips, the two markets would tend toward an equilibrium in which the number of trips supplied equates the cost of a round trip with the revenue derived from it.

In this equilibrium the price of a Here-There trip need bear no necessary relationship to that for a There-Here trip. In general, the greater the demand for the former relative to the latter type of trip, the closer the price for a Here-There trip would be to the total cost of a round trip. Indeed, if the imbalance in demand is sufficiently great, Here-There main-haul trips could end up bearing the entire cost of round trips, while There-Here back-haul trips are provided at a price that covers only pickup and delivery costs. Under such circumstances, the low price of There-Here trips might lead shippers to relocate. Demand schedules would then shift in a fashion tending to equalize the prices of shipments in the two directions. As in the shorter run, however, there would be no reason to expect the two rates to reach exact equality regardless of how much time is allowed to pass.[e]

That a competitively organized transportation market would reach this sort of equilibrium does not, of course, mean that it is always observed in the real world. In the United States, interstate truck and rail rates are typically set by carriers which organize into rate bureaus under the supervision of the Interstate Commerce Commission. The rate structure that these regulated cartels have established for truck transportation between the Midwest and the West Coast is such that empty trailers are typically hauled from West to East. At the same time, however, the rail rate structure is such that empty boxcars are typically hauled from East to West.

THE PEAK LOAD PROBLEM

It will prove useful to distinguish two sorts of variable proportions–joint production situations and to discuss them in rather different ways. In the next section, a production process (sheep raising, again) is dealt with that yields two products at each point in time. This section discusses the simplest "peak load" problem: A single product (widgets, again) cannot be stored. The demand for it varies systematically over time periods of sufficiently short duration that the

---

[e]The analysis of the preceding paragraphs has a very long intellectual history. It was perhaps first presented by Ellet [2] (pp. 130–131) in 1839.

capital plant engaged in producing it cannot be varied so as to keep price and long run marginal cost continuously equal to each other.

Many industries face demand relationships that vary regularly and more or less predictably from hour to hour, day to day, week to week, or season to season—periods of time too short to permit capital stock to be altered. It is convenient to distinguish two groups of these variable demand commodities: those for which storage costs (1) are and (2) are not small enough that variations in finished goods inventories can be used to moderate appreciably the effects on output levels of short term demand variations. This latter group is one to which many transportation activities seem clearly to belong. Analysis of this group is simplified because consumption during each demand period must equal production during that period. This being the case, the existence of a varying inventory of finished goods need not be taken into account.

Suppose that widgets belong to this latter group. Suppose, to be more specific, that the widget industry is competitively organized; that each widget manufacturer produces under the same constant returns to scale cost conditions; that widgets cannot be stored; that the demand for them is substantially greater during the fall and winter than during the spring and summer; and that widget producing capital equipment cannot be employed in other activities and cannot be varied over the demand cycle.[f]

A short run cost function is associated with each widget producer's fixed stock of capital equipment. Two sorts of short run cost relationships can usefully be distinguished—those referred to as Type I and Type II in Chapter Two. With Type I processes (except possibly at low output levels), short run marginal cost is greater than short run average variable cost, and both average and marginal costs increase steadily with output. A limit may or may not exist beyond which output cannot be expanded while holding the capital stock fixed. With Type II cost relationships, short run marginal and average variable costs have the same constant value for all levels of output below plant capacity— the maximum output that can be produced with the fixed capital stock.

If widget production involves a Type I cost relationship, as long as the market price exceeds his minimum average variable cost of production, a profit maximizing (or loss minimizing) widget manufacturer will produce that output in each period for which his short run marginal cost equals the market price. Thus, if the price is P_1 in Figure 6-1 during the fall and winter, he will

---

[f]It is also necessary to assume that only one technology—one production function—exists for the manufacture of widgets. Under normal circumstances, this assumption is unnecessary. If more than one production process exists, that which, given the prices of inputs, involves the lowest costs will automatically be selected. When short run demand variations occur, however, which alternative technology involves the lowest cost will typically depend not just on factor prices but also on how substantially demand varies from period to period. This point is discussed at greater length in the final section of this chapter as it relates to the optimization of highway facilities.

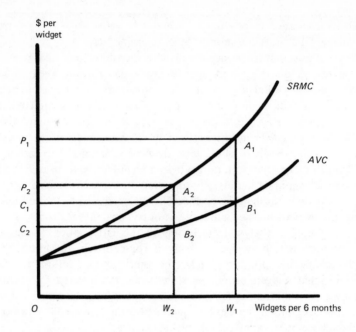

Figure 6-1. Peak Load Equilibrium of Business Firm with Type I Costs

produce W_1 widgets during this peak demand period. Similarly, if the spring-summer market price is P_2, he will establish an off-peak production level of W_2 widgets. If widget production involves a Type II cost relationship and if both the peak and off-peak market prices exceed average variable (and short run marginal) costs, the widget manufacturer will operate at his capacity output level year around. If the price falls to C in Figure 6-2 during the off-peak period, however, he would be indifferent between producing at capacity, producing nothing at all, or producing at any intermediate level. This is true because his revenues will just cover his variable production costs regardless of the output level he establishes.

Regardless of whether Type I or Type II cost relationships apply to widget production, the revenues received by the widget manufacturer in each period can be broken into two parts—variable costs (the *OWBC* areas in Figures 6-1 and 6-2) and quasi-rents (the *PABC* areas). The sum of peak and off-peak period quasi-rents during any particular year need not equal the depreciation and interest costs of widget manufacturing capital plant. If the sum of these quasi-rents exceeds the costs of his capital equipment, the widget producer and others have an incentive to invest in additional widget producing capacity. Doing so would lead to increased output, a lower price, and a reduced quasi-rent in each demand period. The industry will be in long run equilibrium only

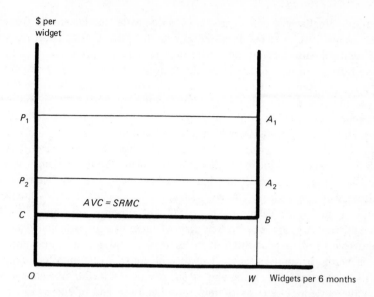

Figure 6-2. Peak Load Equilibrium of Business Firm with Type II Costs

when the sum of the quasi-rents in the two demand periods equals the yearly costs of owning and using capital equipment.

In brief, there is only one appreciable difference between the invariant demand case discussed in Chapter Two and that dealt with here. In defining long run equilibrium, "quasi-rent on invested capital" must be replaced by "the sum of quasi-rents over the demand cycle." Providing that the production process in question is characterized by constant returns to scale, short run marginal cost pricing coupled with an investment program under which capital plant is adjusted to equate the costs of owning and using it with the quasi-rents generated by it would make it unnecessary to worry about allocating overhead costs between the two demand periods.

The reasoning underlying this example of widget production under variable demand conditions can be applied in a straightforward fashion to the highway and public utility peak load problems. As for the highway problem, the only formal difference between widget production and transportation activities are that those who ship goods or travel play a producing as well as consuming role, and that, in the latter of these roles, shippers and travelers vary in the values they place on their self-supplied inputs.

As was argued in Chapters Three and Four, despite these formal differences, highway and other forms of transportation can be analyzed in terms similar to those of any other Type I production process. It follows that, in the absence of scale economies, the existence of variable demands does not imply optimum highway system characteristics that differ fundamentally from those of the competitive industry discussed in Chapter Two. To take short run variations in demand into account, the rules suggested in Chapters Three and Four for optimizing constant returns to scale highways would have to be modified only slightly. It need only be made explicit that the toll required to make each user bear the full short run marginal cost of his trip might differ from one time period to another. A policy of expanding a highway if total toll revenues are greater than capital costs would still be optimal.

Since it involves only replacing "widgets" by "electricity" in the above paragraphs, the cost allocation problem faced by firms—or the commissions that regulate them—that generate and distribute electric power are also easy to deal with.^{g} The costs incurred by an electric utility are commonly broken into three categories (Garfield and Lovejoy [3], pp. 138-139): customer, capacity, and energy. The first of these categories includes such directly allocable fixed costs as those of meter reading and of connecting individual customers to distribution lines. The second consists of capital equipment costs, which are regarded as being almost entirely determined by the annual peak load on the system. The costs of fuel, fuel handling, and of energy losses in transmission lines are the main constituents of the third category. The rate at which these costs are incurred is commonly regarded as proportional to the rate at which energy is consumed; that is, energy cost per kilowatt hour supplied is regarded as independent of the rate at which capacity is utilized.

If the cost relationships involved are, in fact, of this nature, electric power generation and distribution would exhibit Type II cost conditions. In the absence of scale economies, an optimum pricing and investment policy for a firm in this industry could be specified in the following terms: Suppose that, at some point in time, the firm has a generating capacity of E^* kilowatts and that, for outputs below E^*, short run marginal (equals average variable) generation and distribution cost is C^* per kilowatt hour. During some times of day on some days of the year, at a price of C^*, the rate at which electric power would be purchased would fall short of E^*. During these times a price of C^* is appropriate. At other times, a price of C^* would result in energy being demanded at a rate in excess of E^*. At these times prices just high enough to reduce the rate of energy consumption to E^* would be in order.

During the periods when a price of C^* is in effect, sales revenues would, of course, make no contribution to overhead. However, when a price of P is in effect, quasi-rents would be generated at a rate of $(P - C^*)E^*$. If the sum of quasi-rents for all hours in which the firm operates at capacity exceeds the costs of its capital plant, an expansion of its facilities would be desirable.

---

^{g}Essentially the same problem is recognized in regulating firms that transmit and distribute natural gas and is faced although probably not recognized by public authorities and private business firms that provide water supply and sewage disposal services.

If quasi-rents fall short of capital costs, a reduction in plant size would be appropriate. Only in long run equilibrium would quasi-rents just cover capital costs. Just as with the widget industry, there would be no need to undertake a formal allocation of overhead costs to individual user classes.[h]

Actually, there is reason to suppose that electric power generation is not subject to Type II cost conditions. Evidence suggests that, except at quite low output levels, the average variable and short run marginal costs associated with a given generating and distribution network increase steadily with increases in output. A nozzle governed turbine of the sort generally employed in thermal power stations uses approximately 10 percent of its rated steam consumption before any electricity is generated. Approximately 14 percent of rated steam consumption is then required to raise output from zero to 20 percent of rated load. An increase from 80 to 100 percent requires approximately 21 percent of rated steam consumption (see Babcock and Wilcox [9], p. 10.13). Thus, even if the cost of producing a pound of steam is independent of a thermal power station's operating rate, the short run marginal cost of generation is still 50 percent greater at 90 percent than at 10 percent of rated load. Similarly, holding fixed the size and voltage of a transmission line, the energy loss resulting from the line's electrical resistance increases with the square of the rate at which energy is sent through it. For both these reasons, electricity prices equal to the sum of short run marginal generation and distribution costs would result in positive quasi-rents (i.e., positive contributions to overhead) at all except, perhaps, very low outputs.

MUTTON AND WOOL AGAIN: EULER'S THEOREM AND COST ALLOCATION

Fixed coefficient–joint product activities of the sort dealt with in the first section of this chapter are rather rare in the real world. Even if there were only one type of sheep, for example, the wool-mutton output ratio could be altered by varying the age at which sheep are slaughtered. To simplify, sheep raising can be regarded as a process that requires feed and sheep (and time) to produce wool and mutton. Suppose, for the moment, that a sheep rancher has decided to produce the specific quantities, W_o and M_o, of wool and mutton respectively each year. He knows that these quantities can be produced with alternative

---

[h]It is perhaps worth noting that this conclusion seems to be at variance with that reached by Steiner [7, 8], Hirshleifer [5], and others who have discussed the peak load problem. Hirshleifer, for example, concluded, (p. 462); "It is clear that any pricing principle based upon allocating . . . total capacity costs will not, except in special cases, be consistent with efficient prices in terms of the marginal conditions." His conclusion may very well be correct. However, the culprit is not short run variations in demand but rather a level of capital investment unequal to the long run optimum level or something other than constant returns to scale.

combinations of animals and feed. If so, he would presumably strive for that combination of inputs that would minimize his total costs.

Suppose that he is currently employing F_o pounds of feed a year with a flock of S_o sheep and that, if he adds one more sheep to his flock, he will be able to reduce his purchases of feed by f pounds a year whild still maintaining annual output at W_o and M_o. If the cost of f pounds of feed is more than the annual cost of adding one sheep to his flock, he could reduce his total costs by increasing his flock. Indeed, he could continue to reduce costs by substituting sheep for feed in this fashion until the saving in feed costs resulting from adding an additional sheep is just offset by the cost of that sheep. Operating with this combination of inputs involves equating the ratio of the price of a sheep to that of a pound of feed with the number of pounds of feed that would be saved by employing one more sheep while continuing to produce the given quantities of mutton and wool. That is, cost minimization would require setting the rate at which sheep and feed can be substituted for each other in the production of W_o and M_o pounds, respectively, of wool and mutton equal to the rate at which these two inputs can be traded for each other in the marketplace—the ratio of their prices.

Suppose that the rancher has found the flock size and feed input rate that satisfies this condition for the wool and mutton outputs in which he is interested, and that the total cost of this combination is C_o dollars. In principle, he could go through the same calculations for every other possible combination of wool and mutton outputs. The result would be a cost function, $C = g(W,M)$, showing the minimum total cost of producing any given pair, W and M, of wool and mutton outputs each year. This cost function would be called "homogeneous of order n" if

$$g(kW, kM) = k^n g(W,M) \qquad (6\text{-}1)$$

If producing W_o pounds of wool and M_o pounds of mutton a year costs C_o dollars, equation (6-1) says that increasing output rates to kW_o and kM_o would result in total costs of $k^n C_o$. Thus, if n equals one-half, quadrupling output rates would lead to a $4^{1/2} = 2$-fold increase in annual costs. Such a value of n implies increasing returns to scale. Since a 4-fold increase in output yields a less than 4-fold increase in total costs, it involves a reduction in average costs, regardless of the proportions in which total costs are allocated between mutton and wool. Any value of n less than 1 would yield similar results: A simultaneous k-fold increase in both wool and mutton output rates would cause less than a k-fold increase in total costs and hence a reduction in unit costs. With n greater than 1, decreasing returns to scale are implied. That is, doubling each output rate would lead to more than a doubling of total costs and hence to an increase in unit costs. Finally, having n equal to 1 can be seen to imply constant returns to scale. With *n* equal to 1, a simultaneous doubling of wool and mutton output would precisely double total costs and similarly with any other value of *k*.

Among the many contributions of the distinguished eighteenth century Swiss mathematician, Leonhard Euler, is one that has come to be called "Euler's theorem on homogeneous functions."[i] In the context of this discussion, it says that, if the sheep ranching cost function is homogeneous of order *n* in the output of wool and mutton

$$nC = W \, \partial f / \partial W + M \, \partial f / \partial M \qquad (6\text{-}2)$$

In this expression, $\partial f / \partial W$ is the change in total costs that would result from a one-pound increase in annual wool output if mutton output is held fixed. A similar interpretation applies to $\partial f / \partial M$; that is, $\partial f / \partial W$ is the marginal cost of wool and $\partial f / \partial M$ is the marginal cost of mutton. Equation (6-2) says that if wool output *W*, times its marginal cost, is added to mutton output *M*, times its marginal cost, the result will equal *n* times the total cost of producing *W* pounds of wool and *M* pounds of mutton a year. If *n* is less than 1—i.e., if sheep ranching involves increasing returns to scale—wool output times the marginal cost of a pound of wool, plus mutton output times the marginal cost of a pound of mutton, will add to less than total annual costs. With decreasing returns to scale (*n* greater than 1) the sum of these two products will exceed total costs.

Finally, with constant returns to scale, wool output times its marginal cost, plus mutton output times its marginal cost, will equal precisely the total costs of the inputs required to produce these products. Under these circumstances, if a sheep rancher receives a price equal to its marginal cost for each pound of wool and mutton he produces, his operation would just break even: his total revenues would just suffice to cover his total costs. No residual or overhead or joint or common costs would remain to be allocated. These conclusions apply to any productive activity, not just to this simplified sheep grazing process. Thus, the discussion could just as well have been developed in terms of labor, machines, widgets, and gizmoes as in terms of sheep, feed, wool, and mutton. Furthermore, any number of inputs or of outputs could have been considered.

In brief, regardless of the number of inputs and outputs involved, if (1) a production process is characterized by constant returns to scale[j] and the

---

[i]For a proof and a more general expression of Euler's theorem, see Allen [1], pp. 315–320.

[j]Suppose that the function $h(F, S, W, M) = 0$ shows the alternative combinations of annual wool (*W*) and mutton (*M*) output that can be produced with *F* pounds of food and a flock of *S* sheep. This production process would be characterized by constant returns to scale if $h(kF, kS, kW, kM) = 0$ for all positive values of *k*.

possibility of substituting among inputs and outputs, (2) the combination of inputs is selected that minimizes the costs of whatever bundle of outputs is settled upon, and (3) a price equal to its marginal cost is collected for each unit of each output, then the total revenues derived from the sale of process outputs *exactly* equal the total costs of process inputs. The problem of allocating joint or common or overhead costs simply would not arise.

So far, all that has been shown is that if sheep raising is characterized by constant returns to scale, and if the prices of wool and mutton happen to be exactly equal to their marginal costs, then revenues will equal costs. Nothing has been said as yet about the way in which the wool and mutton markets come into equilibrium. Suppose that a sheep rancher has selected a wool-mutton output ratio for which the marginal cost of mutton equals its market price but for which the marginal cost of wool happens to be less than its market price. Clearly he would then have an incentive to expand wool output. One way of doing this would be to adjust his slaughtering and feeding schedules so as to increase his wool-mutton output ratio. Under normal circumstances such a change would serve both to increase the marginal cost of wool and to reduce that of mutton—thus price would exceed marginal cost for both commodities. He and other ranchers would therefore have an incentive to expand their purchases of sheep and feed thereby increasing the supplies of both products and hence reducing their prices. Ultimately, an equilibrium would be reached in which the marginal cost of each product equaled its market price.

The process of adjustment for the variable output proportions case, then, is quite similar to that for the fixed output proportions case. In particular, price equals marginal cost for each commodity simultaneously is a necessary condition for both types of activity to be in equilibrium. If each is in this sort of equilibrium, total revenues will just cover total costs; again, no residual of joint costs will remain to be allocated.

THE HIGHWAY COST ALLOCATION PROBLEM
AND ALTERNATIVE TECHNOLOGIES

The approaches that have been used to allocate the costs of highway improvements among groups of highway users fall into two broad groups. On the one hand it has been argued that the benefits provided by highway improvements differ from user group to user group and that an equitable allocation of costs would dictate establishing charges proportionate to benefits received. On the other hand it has been argued that equity dictates assessing each user group only for the costs occasioned by it.

As was suggested in the introduction to this chapter, the problems involved in this latter approach are commonly discussed in the following manner: If a highway is constructed to serve only passenger vehicles, its pavement need not be as thick as would be the case if it must also serve heavy trucks. Truck owners clearly cause (and hence ought to bear) full financial responsibility for the costs of the extra pavement required to carry their vehicles. In addition, they ought to bear a "fair share" (unfortunately, an ambiguous concept) of the pavement costs that would, in any event, be required to serve private passenger vehicles. The Highway Revenue Act of 1956 both established the Interstate Highway System in the United States and led to considerable research aimed at quantifying both these approaches, i.e., to determining both the differential benefits and the incremental pavement and other costs associated with individual vehicle classes.[k] Unfortunately, this research is of only indirect relevance to achieving an optimum utilization of a given highway network or to determining the optimum capacity for the network.

Referring again to Chapter Three, achieving a benefit maximizing or efficient or optimum utilization of any highway network would require levying a toll on each user. This toll would equal the difference between the short run marginal cost of each user's trip and those costs he himself bears in taking it. The toll would reflect both those maintenance and perhaps other costs that his trip imposes on the public authority providing the highway and the costs he imposes on other users by increasing congestion on the highway. Optimizing the use of a highway would require levying different tolls on different users only to the degree that their trips involve different congestion or maintenance costs. Recognizing the existence of different user classes in no way alters the fundamental conclusion reached in Chapter Three regarding the size of an optimum highway. Given constant returns to scale, the part of short run marginal cost toll collections that reflects congestion on an efficiently designed highway—i.e., the quasi-rent on its capacity—would just cover the capital costs of providing it.

That both the optimum capacity and the optimum pricing system for a highway can be characterized without reference to either differential benefits or incremental pavement costs by no means indicates that research on these topics is pointless. Chapter Three's analysis assumed, for simplicity, that the only attribute of a highway is its capacity. Clearly, highways have many other dimensions, such as pavement type and thickness, grade and curvature standards, and presence or lack of controlled access, to name just a few. Variations in these characteristics can substantially affect the short run marginal costs of trips at any given volume-capacity ratio. Thus an increase in pavement thickness may reduce maintenance costs, particularly those associated with heavy trucks. Similarly, reducing a highway's average rate of rise and fall may reduce both the time and the vehicle operating costs of a trip—again, particularly for heavy trucks. Elimination of an intersection at grade would not only increase the capacity of a given stretch of concrete but would also increase the average speed

[k]For a comprehensive summary of this research, see U.S. Bureau of Public Roads [11].

attainable at any given volume-capacity ratio. Each of these changes would, of course, also increase the cost of a unit of highway capacity.

If the present value of the savings anticipated from an improvement exceed its costs, it would usually be desirable to undertake it. The pavement on a road should be made thicker as long as the incremental cost of doing so falls short of the resulting reduction in the present value of future maintenance outlays. Similarly, if the capital outlays required to make a road less hilly lead to a greater offsetting reduction in the present value of future vehicle operating and time costs, more grade reduction would be warranted.

Again, however, each such improvement would increase the cost of a unit of highway capacity. Such improvements would therefore serve to increase the volume-capacity ratio at which quasi-rents would equal capital costs. Nevertheless, regardless of the set of grade, curvature, pavement thickness, and other noncapacity characteristics that are determined to be optimum, the optimum capacity of a constant return to scale highway would be characterized by equality of capital costs and the quasi-rents generated by short run marginal cost prices. Noncapacity characteristics would affect the optimum toll on an optimum size highway only through their effects on the cost of a unit of capacity.

The optimum set of noncapacity characteristics for a highway depends, of course, upon the nature of the traffic that can be expected to flow over it. Thus, as the percentage of heavy trucks comprising a traffic stream increases, the optimum pavement thickness would likely also increase, while the optimum maximum grade would likely decrease. Similarly, the costs of interchanges and overpasses are sufficiently great that a given fixed budget can build substantially more unlimited than limited access highway capacity. Thus, with a given budget it might be possible to build an unlimited access highway between Here and There having the traffic volume–average travel time per trip relationship shown by A in Figure 6-3. With the same budget, a limited access highway with the relationship between these variables shown by B might also be possible. By providing grade separations only at major intersections, still a third relationship, C, might be possible. In general, holding the budget and all characteristics other than number of grade separations constant, the maximum speed attainable on the road can be increased only by sacrificing capacity.

Which of the travel time–volume relationships obtainable with a fixed budget is "best" depends upon the characteristics of the traffic flowing between Here and There. In particular, as the variability of the traffic stream being considered increases, it becomes more desirable to sacrifice high maximum attainable speeds for high capacities. Thus it would generally seem desirable to build roads leading to seasonal resort areas (areas where weekend, in-season traffic is relatively very high but off-season traffic is very low) to lower grade separation standards than those applied to urban highways. Again, however, regardless of the standards ultimately settled upon, an optimum capacity level

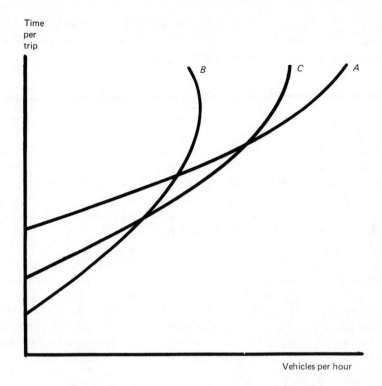

Figure 6-3. Alternative Highway Short Run Cost Schedules for a Given Capital Outlay

would (given constant returns to scale) be characterized by equality of quasi-rents and capital costs.

It is also worth noting that although benefits received play no direct role in determining either an optimum pricing system or an optimum capacity for a highway, very real considerations of equity underly the argument that differential benefits ought to play a role in allocating the costs of highway improvements. The nature of this equity issue can perhaps most easily be described by considering two homogeneous groups, trucks and passenger cars, traveling between Here and There. If no indivisibilities or scale economies are involved in highway construction, a tailor-made road should be provided for each user group. Since trucks are larger and impose greater axle loads than cars, the optimum truck road would presumably have both thicker pavements and higher bridge clearances than would the optimum passenger car road. Similarly, since the operating and time costs of trucks increase more rapidly with increases in a road's average rate of rise and fall than is the case with passenger cars, the optimum truck road would also probably involve lower maximum grades. On each of these three counts, then, the cost of a unit of capacity for the truck road would be greater than that for the passenger car road.

But indivisibilities in the provision of roads do exist; and because of them it is rarely economic to construct specialized truck and passenger car roads. A single road is normally built to serve both vehicle groups. Clearly, it would not be possible to establish specifications for a road that are simultaneously optimum for both trucks and cars: some compromise between the two sets of specifications could not be avoided. In general, the greater the ratio of truck to private passenger vehicle traffic, the closer the optimum set of compromise specifications would be to those that would have characterized the tailor-made truck road.

Suppose that noncapacity specifications equal to those that would have characterized a specialized truck road are settled on for the road serving the two groups. The optimum capacity of this road would still be that for which quasi-rents equal capital costs. However, this optimum capacity would involve an element of unfairness to private passenger vehicle operators. Implicit in the tolls which equate their direct costs with the short run marginal costs of their trips would be quasi-rents for bridge clearances they do not use, pavement thicknesses that result in little if any reduction in the maintenance outlays for which they are responsible, and expenditures to reduce grades in excess of those which would, for them, equate marginal capital costs with marginal vehicle operating and time cost savings.

Identical inequities were implicit in Chapter Four's discussion of optimizing the capacity of a highway utilized by drivers who place different values on their travel time. If the capacity of such a road minimizes aggregate travel costs, a driver with a time value substantially below the average is forced to pay a congestion toll reflecting a level of highway capacity that is, for him, too great. Whether this inequity warrants redress is a matter for politicians, not economists, to decide. Nevertheless, to effect compensation for these inequities by adjusting highway user charges would reduce the efficiency with which highway networds are utilized.

Many studies of differential benefits and incremental costs were undertaken in response to the Highway Revenue Act of 1956. These studies generated data from which it should be possible to quantify the inequities that would result from strict reliance on short run marginal cost pricing for highway services. These data would also likely enable the determining of optimum sets of noncapacity characteristics for highways having different traffic patterns and passing through different terrains. Unfortunately, these benefit and cost studies were mainly oriented toward the impossible task of allocating highway construction costs among user groups. Consequently, the resulting published data are not in a form that would facilitate easy application to more relevant problems.

Chapter Seven

The Shapes of Transportation Cost Schedules—Delays, Congestion, and Random Demands

The short run cost curves drawn in economics texts are almost invariably of the sort labeled Type I in Chapter Two. This is, the normal textbook cost relationship is one for which the law of diminishing marginal productivity applies either to the very first unit produced or at least well before output reaches the capacity of the fixed inputs employed. With the law of diminishing marginal productivity operating, successive equal increments of output require successively larger increments of variable inputs; marginal and average variable costs increase with increases in the ratio of output to capacity.

In everyday discussions of manufacturing cost relationships, however, specification of the number of machine and labor hours and the quantity of raw materials required to produce an additional pound of flour, loaf of bread, or widget is commonly not conditioned on the output-capacity ratio. Similar considerations apply to transportation activities. Thus, in enumerating the direct costs of carrying additional carloads of freight between Here and There, only such outlays are commonly considered as those for providing additional fuel and boxcars, and for switching cars to and from trains. These outlays are also normally specified without reference to the rate at which traffic flows.

If the additional outlays for the variable inputs required to produce additional units of product do not increase with the rate at which fixed capital equipment is utilized, then the law of diminishing marginal productivity does not apply. Rather, what Chapter Two labeled Type II production processes are involved. These are processes for which marginal and average costs are equal at least as long as some unutilized capacity exists.

The implicit assumption that some unutilized capacity remains is also common in everyday discussions of cost relationships: a factory can always squeeze out an additional auto or widget; there is always room for an additional car on a train, or an additional train on a track. If a process operates at less than capacity under Type II cost conditions, then prices set equal to short run marginal costs would serve only to cover variable costs. Such prices would yield no contribution to fixed or overhead costs.

As Chapter Six suggested, the combination of Type II cost conditions and less than capacity operation would be inefficient if scale economies and indivisibilities could be ignored. For an activity to operate under such conditions would clearly involve excess capacity. A reduction in invested capital to a level consistent with capacity operation and quasi-rents equal to capital costs would result from the functionings of competitive markets and would also be socially desirable.

It is perhaps easy to conceive an adjustment in electric utility or truck line capacity that would equate quasi-rents with capital costs. The comparable mental exercise is less easy for a railroad, however. After all, if two points are connected by only one railroad track, an adjustment in rail capacity between them might *seem* an impossibility.[a] This being the case, it is important to explore the extent to which railroad and other common carrier costs really are characterized by Type II costs conditions. Such an exploration is the task of this chapter.[b]

THE SHAPE OF A RAILROAD'S
SHORT RUN COST SCHEDULE

Although the fact seems rarely to be recognized,[c] congestion does play an important role in common carrier costs. Just as for a highway, the time required for the average train to travel over the tracks connecting Here and There likely depends on the rate at which other trains use these tracks. Above some perhaps very low level, an increase in the use of a given line would likely result in an increase in the time any one train is forced to spend on a siding. Similarly, with a fixed stock of railroad cars, an increase in the demand for service would reduce the probability of an empty car's being immediately available to accommodate a given shipper. The average distance from which an empty car would have to be brought, or the average time required to fill an order, or both, would therefore increase. The former effect would increase the cost to the railroad of providing service; the latter would not do so. However, it would affect service

---

[a]"Seem" is italicized because the capacity of a railroad track is far from a fixed number. By adjusting grades and curves, using heavier or lighter rails and more or less elaborate control and signal devices, and by varying the number of sidings, the capacity of a single rail line can be adjusted over a broad range.

[b]Increasing returns to scale are associated with a number of the phenomena dealt with in this chapter. Discussions of their scale economy aspects will be deferred to Chapter Twelve.

[c]An excellent study in which these costs are analyzed is Beckmann, McGuire, and Winsten [1]. Much of the discussion that follows is based on pages 139–156 of this book.

quality and hence the price differential at which a shipper would be indifferent between rail and truck services.

Actually, much more of the time that elapses between departure of a railroad car from a shipper's loading dock and arrival at its destination is spent in railroad classification yards then in movement over rail lines.[d] The operations that take place in a railroad yard can conveniently be broken into three categories: receiving, sorting, and making up. On first arriving in a yard, the cars in a train are separated into one or more groups and stored in a corresponding number of receiving tracks. The couplings, journals, brakes, and other mechanical equipment on each car are then inspected. After inspection of a group has been completed and a "switch list" has been prepared, the group is ready for classification. Classification involves categorizing each car in an incoming group by destination, contents, type, or need for repairs, and then switching it onto one of anywhere from a few to as many as several dozen corresponding classification tracks. Subsequently, etiher on a fixed time schedule or when a specified number has accumulated, the cars on one or more of these tracks are "pulled" by a switch engine to make up an outbound train and taken to a departure track.

In a classification yard studied by Beckmann, McGuire, and Winsten [1], during a two-week period, the daily average of the time that elapsed between arrival of a carload of a nonperishable commodity and its placement on a classification track ranged between 3.0 and 7.9 hours. In addition, before departing for its next destination, the daily average wait on its classification track for one of these cars ranged between 6.6 and 12.3 chours. These substantial waits reflect the existence of delays at each of several stages in the receiving-sorting–making up process. In part, these delays reflect railroad operating policy, and in part, stochastic elements in the demand for railroad services. The longest of them, the wait on a classification track, is primarily a result of operating policy.

There are obvious economies in moving a large number of cars at one time. The longer the train, the lower the engine, crew, and perhaps fuel costs per car moved. At the same time, though, holding fixed the rate at which cars in a particular class enter a yard, the number of this type of cars in an outgoing train can be increased only by increasing the average amount of time these cars spend on a classification track.

Suppose, for example, that cars destined for There arrive at an average rate of n per hour. Suppose also tht the railroad schedules trains so that, on average, they contain N Here-There cars or, alternatively, that it follows a "leave when filled" policy (i.e., dispatches a train to There when N cars have

[d]In the United States, "only two hours and 36 minutes were required to move freight cars their average daily mileage in 1956." Nelson [4], p. 2.

accumulated). Under either policy, the average interval between trains would be N/n hours. The average car would wait half this interval, $N/2n$ hours. Clearly, these "accumulation delays" are costly. The price a railroad pays for a typical boxcar day is, at least to some degree, independent of how far the car travels. Railroads receive no explicit compensation for the time cars spend in classification yards. Furthermore, if the average railroad shipper prefers fast to slow shipments, accumulation delays are costly to him and—more important from the railroad's point of view—increase the rate differential necessary to offset the speed advantage of trucks.

The fact that accumulation delays are costly and that, under either scheduling policy, they are related to the length of train suggests that it is quite meaningful to talk of an optimum train length. Denote by V the combined value of an hour of a boxcar's time to a railroad and its contents' time to a shipper, and by F and S those movement costs (including boxcar and shipper time) that are respectively independent of and proportional to the number of cars in a train. Then the average and marginal costs (given the arrival rate, n) of handling a car from the time it arrives on a classification track to the time it enters the next rail yard on the way to its destination can be written:[e]

$$AC(N, n) = VN/2n + S + F/N \qquad (7\text{-}1)$$

$$MC(N, n) = VN/n + S \qquad (7\text{-}2)$$

If the effects of track congestion on train speeds can be ignored, minimizing the average cost per shipment would require either selecting a train length or scheduling departures so that[f]

$$N = (2nF/V)^{\frac{1}{2}} \qquad (7\text{-}3)$$

To the degree that track congestion does reduce train speeds and is related to the number of trains rather than the number of cars, equation (7-3) understates the optimum train length.

In addition to affecting accumulation delays, train length also affects the time consumed by the inspection and classification operations. Cars can be sorted only one at a time in the order in which they occur in a group. The time required to classify a group is therefore approximately proportional to the number of cars it contains. Nothing prevents more than one car in a group from being inspected at a time; nevertheless, Beckmann, McGuire, and Winsten found

---

[e]Total costs. TC, equal the number of cars in a train, N, times average variable costs. Short run marginal costs equal the change in TC resulting from a change in N, $d(TC)/dN$.

[f]This formula is obtained by differentiating $(AC(N, n)$ with respect to N and setting the resulting expression equal to zero.

a strong positive relationship between length of train and the time interval consumed by the inspection process ([1], pp. 140-142). This relationship between train length and inspection time, as well as the delays that occur while cars wait for inspection and sorting operations, appears at least partially to be the result of congestion phenomena.

The rates at which shippers tender cars to railroads vary seasonally and from day to day. As a result, a railroad that operates exclusively on a "leave when filled" basis would experience irregular intervals between the arrival of trains at a classification yard. Even for railroads that operate exclusively on a fixed timetable, bunched arrivals are frequent and, in addition, the lengths of individual trains vary from day to day. An increase in the rate at which cars or trains enter a yard increases both the average amount of switching time required to place a train on an inspection track and the chance that a track will not immediately be available. Similarly, an increase in the rate at which traffic enters increases the probability that one or more classification tracks will be fully utilized.

The existence of irregularities in the rates at which shipment arrive at a classification yard makes delays almost inevitable, except perhaps at very low traffic levels. This is true even if capacity constraints are not encountered on receiving or classification tracks. At least in the short run, the number of inspectors and of switch engines and crews available in a yard is fixed. The number of inspectors available determines the maximum rate at which cars can be inspected. Similarly, the number of switch engines and the geometry of the yard determine the maximum rate at which cars can be classified. If the rate at which cars arrive during some short time intervals exceeds either the switching or inspecting maximum, some cars must wait to have these services performed. The probability that queues of this nature will form is positive, even for average arrival rates well below inspection and classification capacity. Furthermore, the average time a car is delayed in these queues increases at an increasing rate as the average arrival rate approaches the capacity of these operations.

In brief, railroad activities are characterized by Type I, not Type II cost relationships; that is, short run marginal cost exceeds average variable cost even for output levels substantially below capacity. In the short run, an additional shipment entering a classification yard or being hauled by a trail will, on the average, delay other shipments even when operations occur at substantially below capacity levels. These delays impose costs on both railroads and shippers, costs that increase at an increasing rate as the level of shipments approaches capacity. A short run marginal cost price for a railroad shipment would therefore include more than the directly assignable out-of-pocket expenditures for fuel, switch engine services, box car time, and the like. It would also include the cost of the delays imposed by the shipment on the railroad and other shippers. This latter component of a short run marginal cost price would play a role identical to that of the quasi-rent on invested capital generated by short run marginal cost prices for widgets, electric power, or highway trips. In the absence of scale economies, if the stock of railroad cars, the sizes of inspection crews, and the capacities of railroad lines and yards were adjusted so as to equate their costs with the quasi-rents generated by them, not only would revenues equal costs but also a long run optimum level of railroad services would be achieved.

The considerations which led to the "square root" principle described by equation (7-3) can readily be generalized to other forms of common carrier transportation. Thus a substantial fraction of the journey time of those who use urban mass transit systems involves waiting for buses or subway cars to come. Waiting time is costly to most of these travelers. That is, they would be willing to pay money to reduce it. If an average of n travelers per hour desire service and buses are scheduled so as, on average, to carry N travelers, the interval between buses is N/n hours. If travelers do not know the bus schedule, they must, on average, wait half this interval for service to come. The average waiting time per passenger would then be $N/2n$ hours. This being the case, the cost of an average bus trip can be written in precisely the same form as equation (7-1):[g]

$$AC = VN/2n + S + F/N \qquad (7\text{-}4)$$

where V is the value to the average passenger of an hour's waiting time, S is those trip costs (the value of passenger travel time, in particular) that are directly related to the number of passengers carried, and F is those costs (bus driver wages, in particular) that are independent of the number of passengers carried. With this redefinition of symbols, the cost minimizing number of passengers per bus can be found by evaluating equation (7-3).

RANDOM DEMANDS AND INDIVISIBILITIES

The argument that railroad cost relationships are not, in fact, of the Type II or fixed coefficients variety rested to a considerable degree on the assumed existence of an element of randomness in the arrival of box cars or railroad trains at a classification yard. Most of the discussion in preceding chapters and, more generally, most textbook discussions of market behavior explicitly or implicitly assume that the rate at which a commodity will be consumed is exactly determined once it price is set. The assumption of exactly predictable demands is clearly unrealistic for many if not most commodities. Even taking fully into account seasonal, diurnal, and other predictable sources of demand variations through time, some more or less substantial stochastic elements frequently remain.

---

[g]This formulation ignores the fact that the speed at which a bus traverses a route decreases with increases in the number of passengers it carries. See Chapter Twelve.

The existence of random variations in demand give rise to problems when discontinuities exist in cost relationships. These problems have been cited as arguments against marginal cost pricing for transportation and other activities. The following parable suggests the reasoning involved.[h]

> Eastern Airlines provides a shuttle service between Boston, New York, and Washington. No reservation for space on these flights is required. Eastern guarantees a seat at the scheduled time for all who demand service. If the number of passengers arriving for a particular flight exceeds its capacity, a second, standby plane is called into service. What, then, is the marginal cost of serving a passenger on, say, the 9 a.m. Wednesday Boston to New York shuttle? If, on one Wednesday, an empty seat is availabile, the marginal cost of serving the last passenger arriving for this flight would be quite small. If, on the next Wednesday, the last passenger arrives to find no empty seat on the scheduled plane, the marginal cost of serving him would be the full cost of dispatching the standby aircraft. In this sort of situation, a policy of setting prices equal to short run marginal costs would lead to extreme, unpredictable, and clearly undesirable price variations.

Under such circumstances it is useful to introduce the concepts of "expected demand" and "expected costs" (see Walters [5]). The expected demand for a commodity at a price of P is simply the average rate—say D^*—at which it would be sold at that price. Suppose, as in the Eastern Airlines example, that production during a time period must equal the quantity actually demanded during that period. Then the expected cost of D^*—call it C^*—can be found by first multiplying the cost of producing each possible quantity by the probability of that quantity's being demanded (given that the expected demand is D^*), and then summing these products over all possible output levels. The "marginal expected cost", then, is $\Delta C^*/\Delta D^*$. This is the change in expected costs divided by the change in expected demand that brought it about. Even though the marginal cost of producing exactly D units might be zero, the marginal *expected* cost of D need not be zero.

Consider such events as the number of individuals who arrive at a supermarket checkout counter during successive 10-minute intervals, the number of individuals who request copies of the *New York Times* at a particular newsstand on successive Sundays, the number of typewriters in a large office that require repairs during successive weeks, the number of calls processed by a telephone exchange during successive 10-minute intervals, and, to cite a classic statistics textbook example, the number of Prussian soldiers killed annually during the mid nineteenth century from being kicked by horses. All these events

[h]This problem is a variant of the "traveler to Callais paradox" (see Dessus [2]).

seem to be characterized by what can be termed "individual and collective randomness." For example, the probability that one customer will ask for a Sunday *New York Times* is unaffected either by whether any other specific individual seeks a copy or by the total number of individuals who ask for them.

If an event occurs individually and collectively at random, it can be shown that a Poisson frequency distribution describes it.[i] That is, the frequency with which x events (e.g., x *New York Times* customers per Sunday or x deaths from horse kicks per year) occur is given by

$$P(x) = e^{-m} m^x/x! \quad \text{for} \quad x = 0, 1, 2, \ldots \infty$$

in which the parameter m is the average number of events that occur, e is the base of the natural logarithms, $2.71828 \ldots$, and, e.g., $4! = 4 \times 3 \times 2 \times 1$.

To stay with the Eastern Airlines example, the number of individuals who demand seats on the 9:00 a.m. Wednesday flight is the sort of event characterized by the Poisson distribution. To make the calculations simple, suppose that, on average, four people demand seats on this flight and that service must be provided in six passenger planes at a cost of F dollars per flight that is independent of the number of passengers carried. If four people actually demand seats every Wednesday, then the total and marginal costs of providing the service would be F and zero respectively. However, if the demand for seats on this flight does in fact follow the Poisson distribution with $m = D^* = 4$, then *exactly* four people will demand seats only about 19.6 percent of the time. On about 1.8 percent of all Wednesdays, no people will arrive. Between one and six people will arrive 87.1 percent of the time, and between seven and twelve people 11.1 percent of the time. More than twelve people will arrive with sufficient rarity that this possibility can be ignored.

Clearly, if no people arrive on a given Wednesday, no plane need be sent, and no costs will be incurred. If from one to six people arrive, one plane must be dispatched at a cost of F, and if from seven to twelve people arrive, two planes must be sent at a cost of $2F$. The expected total cost of providing the 9 a.m. Wednesday service, then, is

$$C^* = 0.018 \times 0 + 0.871 \times F + 0.111 \times 2F = 1.093F$$

---

[i]The Poisson distribution is commonly developed as a limiting form of the binomial distribution. For a development more nearly in the spirit of this discussion, see Feller [3], pp. 146-149. The fact that all individuals may be influenced by the same general set of circumstances in deciding whether to take an action does not violate the condition's being "collectively at random." What is important is that an individual decision maker not be influenced directly by the actual number of individuals who take the action under analysis. If individuals who enter a supermarket are discouraged from shopping by long queues at the checkout counter, the process is not "collectively at random."

If the price of trips is increased sufficiently to reduce D^* to 3.8, the frequencies with which no, one, and two planes must be sent will change to 2.2, 88.7, and 9.1 percent of the time, respectively, and the expected total cost of providing the service will decline to $C^* = 1.069F$. The marginal expected cost would be $\Delta C^*/\Delta D^* = (1.093F - 1.069F) / (4 - 3.8) = 0.12F$.

In brief, when demand relationships are characterized by stochastic elements, it becomes apparent that while the marginal cost of producing at a given level may be zero, the marginal expected cost of producing at that expected level need not be zero. This conclusion can readily be generalized to any situation in which demand is to some degree random and Type II cost conditions prevail. Suppose, for example, that electric power generation and distribution is a Type II process. Suppose also that marginal and average variable costs would be equal at a particular level of output. Even under these circumstances, charging a price equal to marginal expected cost at that expected output level would still likely yield some contribution to overhead or fixed costs.

Chapter Eight

Measuring the Benefits of Transportation System Investment Projects

Major investment projects by public agencies or private business firms typically have widespread ramifications. Restricting attention to public investments, a multipurpose dam constructed by the U.S. Army's Corps of Engineers can result, among other things, in lower cost electric power, a reduction in flood damages incurred by downstream residents, an increase in the output of farms for which the dam provides irrigation water, and the construction of factories to process this increased farm output. Similarly, obvious causal relationships are involved in construction of a major shopping center near a freeway interchange and in the increases in land values that occur when completion of an expressway reduces the time required to travel from a remote suburb to the central business district of an urban area.

Federal and state laws governing expenditures on roads, dams, and the like typically contain words that say, in effect, "a public investment may be undertaken only if the benefits, to whomsoever they accrue, exceed the costs, whosoever may incur them."[a] This chapter is devoted to describing frameworks that rely directly or indirectly on the concept of consumer's (or consumers') surplus for analyzing the anticipated consequences of a major project to estimate its aggregate benefits and costs as a basis for determining whether this legislative mandate will be satisfied. These analytical frameworks are of equal use in dealing with a dam, a bridge, a steel mill, or any other major public investment. For concreteness, however, the discussion will be concerned mainly with the effects of a proposed improvement in the road between Here and There. Chapter Nine contrasts these consumers' surplus benefit measures with those based on changes in national income, while Chapters Ten and Eleven discuss

[a]Unfortunately, "whosoever may incur them" is all too often ignored in the benefit-cost calculations that are commonly undertaken in response to this legislative mandate. While indirect project benefits are often measured, indirect project costs are usually ignored.

what may seem to be unique effects of transportation investments—effects that may seem to require the use of special analytical techniques and standards of valuation in measuring their benefits and costs.

The discussion of this chapter proceeds in several steps. First to be dealt with is the assignment of a dollar value to the change in a single consumer's utility level that results from changes in the economic environment[b] he confronts. The next steps involve aggregating these dollar measures of benefit across all individuals affected by the change. This aggregation process will be dealt with first under the assumption that a regime of marginal cost pricing prevails throughout the economy. This assumption is particularly unrealistic as it relates to transportation activities. The toll for highway use implicit in gasoline and other highway user charges, for example, is only by accident equal to the toll that would be required to set the price of a trip on a street or highway equal to the marginal cost of that trip. The chapter therefore concludes with a discussion of the problems involved in aggregating benefits when marginal cost prices cannot be assumed to prevail.

MEASURING INDIVIDUAL BENEFITS

Consider an individual who, at some point in time, is confronted by an array of prices, P_1. This array involves not just the prices (including any excise or sales taxes) of commodities he buys but also the net of tax wage rates he would earn for such services as he is capable of performing, the net of tax rental rates on such assets as he may own, and finally, such lump sum grants as he may receive or taxes he may pay.[c] The individual responds to these prices by adjusting his consumption, work, and asset rental activities so as to maximize his utility. Doing so results, among other things, in a total money income of I_1.

Suppose that construction of a dam or road, a change in the demand for his services, or some other event leads to a change in one or more of the prices confronting the individual. His adjustment to this change in his economic environment leads to a situation that can be described by the pair (P_2, I_2). In this pair, at least one of the prices comprising P_2 differs from the corresponding price in P_1, and I_2 may or may not be the same as I_1.

[b]As distinct from which might be termed his "qualitative environment." An expressway, for example, is noisy and smelly. At the same time, however, its construction diverts traffic from other traffic arteries in its vicinity thereby reducing the noises and smells experienced by those who live or do business near these arteries. The benefit implications of these shifts in noises and smells are both important and have effects on the economic environment. The problems involved in placing dollar values on changes in the qualitative environment will not be explored in what follows, however.

[c]A "lump sum" tax or grant is one that an individual pays or receives regardless of what other actions he may take, e.g., regardless of how much or little he works or what commodities he buys or sells.

A variety of dollar measures of the benefit (or loss) to the consumer as a result of the change from (P_1, I_1) to (P_2, I_2) could be (and, indeed, have been) proposed. Among the conceptually simplest of such measures is one that requires information on the individual's demand and supply schedules for those goods and services whose prices have changed between situations 1 and 2. Given this information, it would be possible to determine that income (call it I_1') for which the combination (P_2, I_1') would give him the same utility as the combination (P_1, I_1).[d] This information would also make it possible to determine the combination (P_1, I_2'), which would give the same utility as (P_2, I_2) or, indeed, combinations (P_3, I_1'') and (P_3, I_2''), which respectively would give the same utility as (P_1, I_1) and (P_2, I_2) where P_3 is any other array of prices that may be of interest.

The differences $I_2 - I_1'$, $I_2' - I_1$, and $I_2'' - I_1''$ would then serve as measures of the consumer's gain or loss in real income as a result of the change in his economic environment from state 1 to state 2. "Measures" in the plural, note—unfortunately, these three "real income change" measures would have identical values only under rather special circumstances. However, their values would be quite similar unless the price changes between states 1 and 2 are large, and the goods and services involved in these price changes account for a substantial fraction of the consumer's economic activity, and his income elasticities of demand[e] or supply for them differ substantially from zero.

The real income change measures described in the preceding paragraph are closely related to what have long been referred to as "consumer's surplus" benefit measures. Figure 8-1 depicts a consumer's "normal" demand for widgets—the quantity of widgets he would buy at alternative prices for them if his money income and the prices of all other commodities he buys are held fixed. If the current price of widgets is OF, his widget consumer's surplus is areas AFB. This area equals the sum over all widgets he buys of the difference

---

[d]It can be shown that, if a consumer's utility is to be held fixed, the rate at which his income must change with changes in the price of a commodity equals the quantity of that commodity he consumes. The quantity he buys, in turn, is a function of his income and the commodity's price. In symbols, $dI/dP|_u = X(P,I)$. This expression can be regarded as a first order differential equation. (P_2, I_1') can be determined by solving this equation sequentially for each commodity whose price has changed and using the consumer's initial income and the initial and final prices with which he is confronted to specify the constants of integration that arise. For a fuller development of the process involved and a specific example of the computations, see Mohring [4], pp. 349–355.

[e]Suppose that consumer's income increases but that all of the prices he faces (including that for widgets) remain unchanged. Then his income elasticity of demand for widgets equals the percentage by which his consumption of them changes divided by the associated percentage change in his income. A similar definition applies to the income elasticity of supply for a service rendered by the consumer.

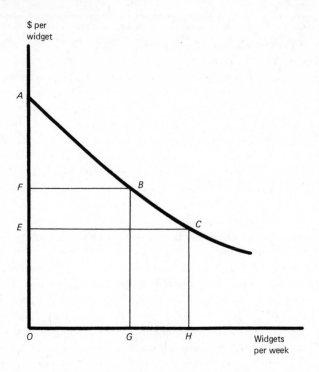

Figure 8-1. Consumer's Surplus

between the price he would be willing to pay for a given widget and the price he actually does pay for that widget.

Suppose the widget consumer is given a choice between (1) continuing to buy *OG* widgets per week at a price of *OF* per widget, and (2) foregoing their consumption entirely. His widget consumer' surplus can be shown to equal approximately the maximum amount of income he would be willing to give up each week to avoid alternative (2).[f] The word "approximately" is necessary because *ABF* would exactly equal the sacrifice that would make him indifferent between no widgets at all and *OG* at a price of *OF* only if his income elasticity of demand for widgets happens to equal zero. If, as is true of most commodities, widgets are a superior good—i.e., one with a positive income elasticity—area *ABF* exceeds the sacrifice he would be willing to make. The magnitude of the over estimate is small, however, unless his income elasticity of demand for widgets is substantially greater than zero and outlays on them account for a substantial share of his total expenditures.

---

[f]For a demonstration of this fact and an extended development of the consumer's surplus concept, see, e.g., Hicks [3], chs. 10 and 18.

Suppose, now, that a very simple change in the consumer's economic environment occurs. The price of widgets falls but all other prices, as well as his money income, remain fixed. As a result, his weekly widget purchases increase from *OG* to *OH* in Figure 8-1 and his widget consumer's surplus increases by *FBCE* per week. For this simple change in the consumer's environment, area *FBCE* is closely related to the "real income change" measures of benefit outlined at the beginning of this section. If widgets are a superior good, the $I_2 - I_1'$ real income change measure[g] is somewhat smaller while the $I_2' - I_1$ measure is somewhat large than *FBCE*. If the consumer's income elasticity of demand for widgets is zero, $I_2 - I_1'$, $I_2' - I_1$, and *FBCE* all have the same value.[h]

AGGREGATING INDIVIDUAL BENEFIT MEASURES

A "Bergsonian social welfare function" is a common theoretical construct in the branch of economic theory referred to as welfare economics. It involves visualizing society as having specified a function, $W = f(u^1, \ldots, u^n)$, which determines an overall index of social well-being, W, from information on the utility levels, $u^1, \ldots, u^n$, of its n individual members. Suppose that society has specified such a function and that an income transfer takes place. Suppose, more specifically, that a dollar is taken away from citizen 1, a rich man, and given to citizen 2, a poor man. The effect of this transfer on the social welfare index, W, can be written:

$$\Delta W = W_2 u_I^2 - W_1 u_I^1 \tag{8-1}$$

In this expression, W_2 is the rate at which social welfare increases when individual 2's utility level increases—his marginal welfare weight, for short. In turn, u_I^2 is the rate at which 2's utility changes when his money income changes—his marginal utility of income, for short. Similar interpretations apply to W_1 and u_I^1.

It seems reasonable to suppose that, on balance, society has egalitarian sentiments—that is, society would place a greater value on a one-unit increase in a poor person's utility than on a one-unit increase in that of a rich person. W_2 would then be greater than W_1. In addition, it is commonly sup-

[g]That is, the measure involving the difference between his after-change income and the income which, at the new price of widgets, would be required to provide his utility level before the price change.

[h]For this simple change in the economy, I_2 is, of course, equal to I_1. The difference between I_2 and I_1' is then equal to what Hicks [3] has called the "compensating variation" of the price change—the amount of income which the consumer would be willing to give up rather than have the price of widgets return to its old, higher level. Similarly, $I_2' - I_1$ is Hick's "equivalent variation"—the amount of income he would have to be given if the price of widgets returns to its old, higher level in order to provide him with the same utility as he derived from his original money income at the new, lower price.

posed that, for most consumers, the marginal utility of income is a diminishing function of income—that is, the richer the consumer, the smaller is the additional utility he would derive from an additional dollar of income.

The change in the economic environment described by equation (8-1) involves taking from the rich and giving to the poor. Therefore, both considerations mentioned in the preceding paragraph suggest that ΔW would be positive unless the transfer has untoward effects on the incentives of the parties involved. Such disincentive effects may well exist: that welfare payments to the poor and higher taxes on the rich result in reduced work incentives for both groups is, after all, a common claim. Be this as it may, analysis of the costs and benefits of government investment projects are almost invariably based on an implicit or explicit premise that serves to set ΔW in equation (8-1) equal to zero. This premise has been labeled "the compensation principle." For the purposes at hand, it can be defined as the assumption that, to society, a dollar is a dollar to whomever it may accrue. Thus, if projects A and B differ only in that A gives individual X \$100 while B gives \$100 to Y, the compensation principle treats society as indifferent between the two projects, regardless of X's and Y's specific identities.[i]

To assume a dollar to a citizen to be a dollar to society regardless of who the citizen may be is, in effect, to assume individual 1's marginal welfare weight, W_1, to equal the reciprocal of his marginal utility of income, u_I^1, and similarly for individual 2. Therefore, if marginal utilities of income are, in fact, diminishing functions of income, the compensation principle is antiegalitarian; i.e., it attaches higher weights to increases in the utility of rich people than to gains by the poor. Many (including myself) regard this attribute of the compensation principle as an important deficiency.[j] Nevertheless, the principle will

---

[i]This definition is not quite equivalent to the compensation principle as it is usually stated—if the gains from a change in the economic environment could be redistributed so as to leave no one worse off while making at least one member of society better off, the change is desirable even if redistribution does not actually take place (see Hicks [2]).

Actually, the definition of the compensation principle given in the text is closer to what is sometimes referred to as the "cost-benefit criterion." Application of this criterion requires, for each individual affected by a change in the economic environment, determining the $I_2 - I_1'$ income change measure described in the first section of this chapter. If the sum of these individual change measures is positive, the cost-benefit criterion is met. Boadway [1] has shown that it is possible for a change to satisfy the cost-benefit criterion test without satisfying the compensation principle test.

[j]For completeness, another deficiency of the compensation principle should be mentioned. It seems reasonable to demand of a social welfare function that the marginal welfare weight for an individual depend only on his utility level and perhaps that of other consumers as well. A consumer's marginal utility of a dollar's worth of income depends, in general, on the prices that confront him as well as on his income. Clearly, if all prices and a consumer's money income double, the value to him of an additional dollar would be cut in half. It would therefore be possible for a consumer to experience a change in income and one or more prices that leaves his utility level unchanged but substantially alters his marginal

be adopted in what follows, for two reasons. First, adoption of a more egalitarian procedure would, at the very least, require information on the income distribution of project beneficiaries—information that is rarely available. Second, if the principle is used only to select among competing projects for which the income distributions of beneficiaries are approximately the same, failure to take income distribution considerations into account would have little practical consequence. Many transportation improvements seem to have this characteristic.

THE CANCELLATION OF BENEFITS AND COSTS
IN AGGREGATING INVESTMENT EFFECTS

Suppose, for concreteness, that improvement of the highway between Here and There is contemplated. Suppose also that a combination of market forces and administrative steps results in equality of the price of each commodity produced in the economy with its marginal cost both before and after the improvement. Price equals marginal cost is assumed to apply, it should be noted, not only in the markets for apples, autos, and widgets, but also for the Here-There road and any other highways that the improvement may affect indirectly. That is, it is assumed that tolls are adjusted on the Here-There and other highways so as to equate the marginal costs of trips with the sum of the dollar and time costs incurred by those who take them.

If undertaken, the improvement will affect prices and output levels in a number of markets. Most obviously, the price of Here-There trips will fall, thereby inducing additional trips to be taken. While the toll per trip on the improved road will likely be smaller than that on the old road, total toll collections by the highway authority may increase or decrease. Those who formerly used nearby roads may find it cheaper to divert parts of their trips to the Here-There road. In addition to benefits they receive as a result, the roads they formerly used will become less congested, thereby lowering the price of trips for those who remain on these roads. The increased accessibility afforded by the improvement will likely serve to increase the values of neighboring residential, commercial, and industrial sites. The lower transportation costs afforded by the improvement will affect not just person trips but also goods shipments. As a result, the delivered price of goods produced Here and sold There will fall.

---

utility of income and hence his marginal welfare weight. This state of affairs leads to the possibility that a change in the economic environment from state 1 to state 2 *and* a change from state 2 back to state 1 would both meet the compensation principle test. This objection to the compensation principle is closely related to that given by Scitovsky [5]. (See Mohring [4], pp. 365–367.) Valid though this objection is, the principle's income distributional implications seem to me to be far more serious. "What's wrong with the compensation principle, Professor Samuelson, sir?" the young graduate student asked with a tug of his forelock. "Compensation isn't paid," the great man replied. "Is that all?" "That's enough."

How should this array of effects be put together to come up with an aggregate benefit measure that can be compared with the improvement's costs to determine whether it should be undertaken? One procedure that could, at least in principle, be followed was suggested in the first section. Consider an individual whose economic environment—i.e., his income or one or more prices—changes as a result of the improvement. His transactions could be examined to determine the income which would be necessary at postimprovement prices to provide the same utility level as he obtained prior to the improvement. The difference between this income and that which he would actually receive after the improvement measures its potential benefit to him. Such a measure could be constructed for each individual affected by the improvement. If the compensation principle is accepted, determining aggregate benefits would merely require adding up these individual benefit measures.

Performing these calculations for projects with widespread ramifications would require an enormous amount of information. It seems clear that, as a practical matter, using this procedure would be impossible for all but the simplest of changes in the economic environment. Fortunately, however, a considerable number of the improvement's effects would tend to cancel each other out. That is, quite frequently, a given effect would involve a benefit to one individual but an at least partially offsetting cost to another. Indeed, if the compensation principle is accepted *and* marginal cost pricing prevails, exact cancellation of virtually all the improvement's effects can be shown to occur. Consumers'[k] surplus geometry is particularly useful in suggesting why this sort of cancellation occurs under these circumstances.

Figure 8-2 depicts the demand schedule for trips by all travelers between Here and There and the short run marginal cost schedules associated with the original highway and a possible improvement involving, say, widening and converting several intersections at grade into cloverleafs. On the old highway, OQ_1 trips take place at a price of OP_1. The net short run[l] benefit derived from these trips by society as a whole can be viewed as the maximum amount travelers would be willing to pay for them, area $OCDQ_1$, minus the actual time and vehicle operating costs incurred in taking them, area $OBDQ_1$. Thus the net short run benefit equals area CBD.

This benefit can be broken into two parts. First is the consumers' surplus benefit of CDP_1. Second is the quasi-rent, P_1DB, generated by the tolls required to equate the full prices of trips with their marginal costs. It should be emphasized that this quasi-rent is just as much a social benefit of these trips as is the

[k]"Consumers'," note, not "consumer's." Acceptance of the compensation principle allows adding up the area under the *market* demand schedule to obtain a measure of aggregate social benefit.

[l]"Short run" referring to the fact that the capital investment in the road is regarded as a sunk cost.

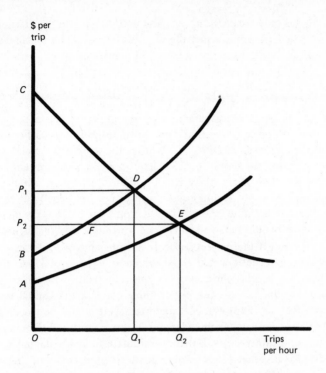

Figure 8-2. Direct Benefits of Road Improvement with Marginal Cost Tolls

consumers' surplus they generate. It is not a benefit captured by consumers but rather one captured by the agency responsible for collecting tolls, and hence, indirectly, by society at large. Society, in turn, can use these tolls to finance public activities for which taxes would otherwise have to be levied.

Undertaking the improvement would change net short run benefits from *CDB* to *CEA* per week. The difference between these two net benefit levels, the area *BDEA*, would be the direct incremental benefit of the improvement. If such effects as the improvement may have on other prices in the economy can be ignored, whether the improvement would be worthwile depends on how area *BDEA* compares with the opportunity cost of the capital investment required to alter the road. If *BDEA* exceeds this hourly capital cost, the improvement would be worthwhile.

As is perhaps apparent from Figure 8-2, the net incremental benefit attributable to the improvement would not, in general, equal the benefit which consumers would derive from using it. This latter benefit is the increase in consumers' surplus resulting from the improvement, area P_1DEP_2. This consumer benefit has only area *FDE* in common with the improvement's net benefit. The consumer benefit would equal the net benefit only if the remainder of consumer benefit, P_1DFP_2, happens to equal the remainder of net benefit, *BFEA*.

Actually, the condition under which the project's consumer and net benefits would be equal has a quite straightforward interpretation. The quasi-rent generated by the highway before its improvement, P_1DB, has area P_2FB in common with the quasi-rent generated after the improvement, area P_2EA. This means that the difference between pre- and postimprovement quasi-rents is equal to the difference between P_1DFP_2 and *BFEA*—the amount by which consumer and project net benefits would differ. Thus, if the same quasi-rent would be generated by the Here-There highway after the improvement as before it, the consumers' surplus benefit would equal the project's net benefit. If the project would increase toll revenues, the net benefit would exceed the consumers' benefit; if toll revenues would fall, consumer benefit would exceed net benefit.

In brief, if the project's effects on other prices in the economy can be ignored, its net benefit would equal the consumers' surplus benefit derived by those who use it, plus the change in the tolls paid by these users. If this potential net benefit exceeds the opportunity costs of the capital investment required to effect the improvement, undertaking it would be worthwhile, unless an alternative investment would yield an even greater difference between benefits and opportunity costs. But is it legitimate to ignore the improvement's potential effects on other prices? Subsequent chapters deal with this question as it relates to changes in land values and to price changes that result from savings in production and distribution costs. Attention here is therefore restricted to such effects as the Here-There improvement may have on trip costs elsewhere in the highway network.

Figure 8-3 depicts the simplest possible example of this sort of effect. Suppose that the Here-There improvement would lead some of those who now use the road between Here and Elsewhere to shift parts of their trips to the Here-There road. More precisely, suppose that these two roads provide substitute products—i.e., that any change that reduces the price of trips on the Here-There road will divert traffic to it from the Here-Elsewhere road and similarly for a change in Here-Elsewhere prices. The demand for Here-There and Here-Elsewhere trips can then respectively be written $D_{HT} = D_1 (P_1, P_2)$ and $D_{HE} = D_2(P_1, P_2)$ where P_1 and P_2 refer respectively to the full prices of Here-There and Here-Elsewhere trips.

Before the improvement, traffic on the two roads is in equilibrium at full prices (direct user costs plus marginal cost tolls) of P_1^* and P_2^*. These are the prices at which consistent demand and marginal cost schedules simultaneously intersect on the two roads. In this context, "consistent" intersections involve $D_1(P_1^*, P_2^*) = MC_1$ and, simultaneously, $D_2(P_1^*, P_2^*) = MC_2$. An improvement such as that shown in Figure 8-2 is then made to the Here-There road, and as a result, the marginal cost price of Here-There trips falls. This reduction leads both to additional trips by former Here-There travelers and to diversion of trips formerly made on the Here-Elsewhere road. This trip diversion reduces the price of trips on the Here-Elsewhere road and hence leads to reverse diversion, i.e., to a shifting to the Here-Elsewhere road of trips formerly made on the Here-There road. This shifting back and forth ultimately results in a new equilibrium on the two roads at prices of P_1^{**} and P_2^{**}.

The economics literature suggests several alternative candidates as measures of consumer benefit under conditions such as those depicted in Figure 8-3. The alternative of greatest value in this discussion can be described in the following terms. Visualize the price of Here-There trips as shifting downward, not once and for all but rather in a series of very small steps. Each of these small price reductions determines a new, lower equilibrium price of Here-Elsewhere trips; that is, the price of Here-Elsewhere trips can be viewed as a function, $P_2(P_1)$, of the price of Here-There trips. Using this function to replace P_2 in the demand schedule for Here-There trips would result in a line like BD in Figure 8-3. Using this same function to replace P_2 in the demand schedule for Here-Elsewhere trips would lead to a line like bd in this figure—i.e., to a "demand schedule" for Here-Elsewhere trips that is superimposed on that road's marginal cost schedule.

With these two demand schedules, area $P_1^* BDP_1^{**}$ in Figure 8-3 is the consumer benefit the improvement confers on Here-There road users, while $P_2^* bdP_2^{**}$ is the indirect benefit derived by travelers on the Here-Elsewhere road.[m] At the same time, however, $P_2^* bdP_2^{**}$ is also the amount by which quasi-rents (toll collections) on the Here-Elsewhere road decline as a result of traffic diversion to the improved road. This means that the gain to Here-Elsewhere users can be ignored in determining the improvement's total benefits. While $P_2^* bdP_2^{**}$ is indeed a benefit to these travelers, this benefit reflects the transfer to users of an income stream that was formerly collected by society at large in the form of tax revenues. This benefit is therefore *not* a gain to society that should be added to that resulting directly from the Here-There improvement.

[m]Alternative measures of consumer benefit are the areas (a) $P_1^* ADP_1^{**}$ plus $P_2^* bcP_2^{**}$ and (b) $P_1^* BCP_1^{**}$ and $P_2^* adP_2^{**}$. Alternative (a) involves determining the area under the demand schedule for Here-There trips when the price of Here-Elsewhere trips is that associated with the *improved* Here-There road plus the area under the Here-Elsewhere demand schedule when the price of Here-There trips is that associated with the *unimproved* Here-There road. Alternative (b) involves the same sort of procedure but with the positions of *improved* and *unimproved* reversed in the preceding sentence.

If the demand for trips on each road is a function only of trip prices, then each of these three measures will have the same numerical value. However, if the number of trips a representative consumer would take between Here and There depends not just on the prices of Here-There and Here-Elsewhere trips but also on the consumer's income, these three measures would turn out to have somewhat different values. Technically, each of these measures involves evaluation of a "line integral" along a different path. In general, the value of a line integral will be independent of the path followed only if certain "integrability conditions" are satisfied. These conditions would be satisfied if trip demands are independent of income but not otherwise.

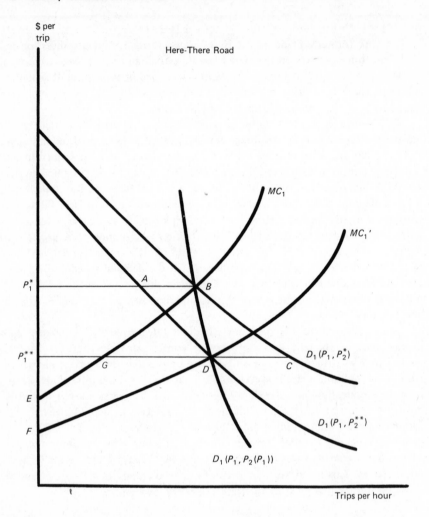

Figure 8-3. Direct and Indirect Effects of Road Improvement with Marginal Cost Tolls

To compare the geometry of Figure 8-3 to that of 8-2, the sum of areas $P_1^* B D P_1^{**}$ and $P_2^* b d P_2^{**}$ in the more complicated situation is the equivalent of $P_1 DEP_2$ in the simpler situation. Of the total consumer benefit, $P_1 DFP_2$ in Figure 8-2, and $P_1^* BGP_1^{**}$ plus $P_2^* bdP_2^{**}$ in Figure 8-3 is the result of a transfer to road users of benefits formerly received by society at large in the form of toll revenues. The basic net short run benefit of the Figure 8-3 improvement is area $EBDF$, the equivalent of $BDEA$ in Figure 8-2.

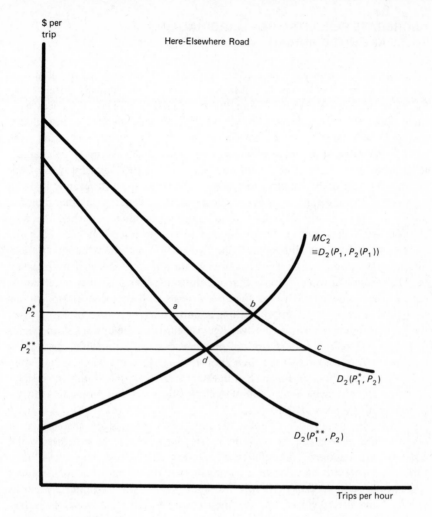

$ per trip

Here-Elsewhere Road

MC_2
$\equiv D_2(P_1, P_2(P_1))$

P_2^*

a

b

P_2^{**}

c

d

$D_2(P_1^*, P_2)$

$D_2(P_1^{**}, P_2)$

Trips per hour

To summarize, if marginal cost tolls are charged for trips, and if the compensation principle is accepted, then determining the net short run benefits of improving a highway link requires only data on the use made of that link. Specifically, the benefit equals the sum of the change in consumers' surplus and toll revenues on the improved link. This is true even if the improvement affects traffic conditions on other links in the system. Given marginal cost pricing and the compensation principle, changes in consumer benefits and toll revenues on unaltered links would exactly offset each other.

AGGREGATE BENEFITS WHEN MARGINAL COST
TOLLS ARE NOT CHARGED

"If marginal cost tolls are charged for trips" is, unfortunately, a critical qualification. In the United States, actual highway user charges normally differ—often by quite substantial amounts—from those required to equate trip prices with their associated marginal costs. As a result, the benefits derived from highway use are lower than they could be. Also, the problems involved in measuring these benefits are greater than those which arise when marginal cost prices are charged. Regardless of the level at which tolls are set, the benefit of a highway improvement is the sum of the changes in consumers' surplus and toll revenue benefits to which that improvement gives rise. However, these benefits on other than the improved road cannot be relied on to cancel each other out when the tolls charged are different from those required to equate price and marginal cost.

It is worthwhile considering two sorts of situations in which prices differ from marginal costs. The first is when no toll at all is levied for highway use. The second is when a toll is charged, but one other than that necessary to equate price and marginal cost. Figure 8-4 deals with the benefit implications of zero user charges. Its interpretation is quite similar to that of Figure 8-3, the basic difference between the two figures being that the upward sloping lines in Figure 8-3 refer to the short run *marginal* costs of trips while the corresponding lines in Figure 8-4 are their short-run *average* costs. That is, the Figure 8-3 lines include but the Figure 8-4 lines exclude the costs an individual Here-There or Here-Elsewhere trip imposes on all other travelers by adding to the level of congestion on these roads.

In the absence of tolls, the only costs incurred by a consumer in taking a trip are his vehicle operating costs and the value he attaches to the time the trip requires. The equilibrium number of trips on each road is therefore that for which the value of a trip to the last traveler just equals the direct costs he incurs in taking it. Before the improvement these equilibria occur at points B and b respectively on the Here-There and Here-Elsewhere roads. Net consumer benefits on the two roads are therefore areas ABP_1^* and abP_2^*. Since no road user charges are assumed to be imposed, these consumer benefits are the total benefits to society from use of the two roads.

Through a process identical to that discussed in describing Figure 8-3, improvement of the Here-There road would lead to new equilibrium travel rates at points D and d respectively for the Here-There and Here-Elsewhere roads. As with Figure 8-3, a variety of consumer benefit measures with approximately equal values could be described for the shift from B and b to D and d. As before, the measure of greatest interest is the sum of $P_1^* BD P_1^{**}$ on the Here-There road and $P_2^* bd P_2^{**}$ on the Here-Elsewhere road. As with Figure 8-3, construction of this benefit measure involves viewing the price of Here-Elsewhere trips as a function, $P_2(P_1)$, of the price of Here-There trips. The resulting demand schedule for Here-There trips is $D_1[P_1, P_2(P_1)]$, while that for Here-Elsewhere trips is superimposed on the average cost schedule for these trips. Unlike the situation with Figure 8-3, however, the benefit to Here-Elsewhere road users is a net benefit of the improvement. Since no tolls are collected, this benefit does not reflect a transfer to users of an income stream formerly received by society at large.

To summarize, if no tolls are charged for trips, determining the net short run benefits of improving one link on a highway system requires information on the effects of that improvement on the use of all other links in the network. Specifically, the benefit equals the sum over all affected links of the changes in consumers' surplus benefits induced by the improvement.

In the United States, the basic "toll" for highway use is that implicit in federal and state gasoline taxes and other excises that are related to the rates at which vehicles are operated. For the use of expressways, these taxes work out to roughly 1 cent per private passenger vehicle mile, regardless of traffic conditions. If the occupants of the average private passenger vehicle value their time at $1.55 an hour, 1 cent per mile is approximately the cost any given expressway trip imposes on other expressway travelers only when the volume-capacity ratio on the expressway is about 50 percent. For a volume-capacity ratio of 90 percent, an expressway toll on the order of 3.7 cents per vehicle mile would be required to equate the price of a trip with its marginal cost, while for a 10 percent volume-capacity ratio, a toll of about 0.1 cents would be appropriate. The corresponding optimum tolls for travel on city streets are 0.4, 2.9, and 11.7 cents for respective volume-capacity ratios of 0.1, 0.5, and 0.9.[n]

To repeat, regardless of the toll levels set, an improvement's net benefit equals the sum of the changes in consumers' surplus and toll revenue benefits to which it gives rise. It would therefore be possible to measure net benefits when price and marginal cost are unequal simply by adding up these changes for all affected highway links. The computational burden involved would be substantial, of course. This computational burden can be reduced somewhat and additional insights into the economic processes involved can be obtained by employing "dead-weight loss" geometry.

Figure 8-5 describes a single one-mile highway when the marginal cost toll exceeds that actually charged. With a marginal cost toll of KE per trip mile, OL trips per hour would be taken. Total hourly benefits of FEJ would result. Of this total, traveler benefits would equal FEG while highway tolls or rents would equal GEJ. However, if a toll of only $BC-1$ cent per vehicle mile,

[n]The expressway numbers (in minutes per mile) were developed along the lines outlined in Chapter Three through use of a travel time (T) — volume-capacity (N/K) relationship similar to that on which Table 3–1 and Figure 3–1 were based. It is: $T = 2 - (1 - N/K)^{1/2}$. This relationship implies speeds of 60 and 30 miles per hour at volume-capacity ratios of zero and one respectively. The city street values are those underlying Figure 3–1.

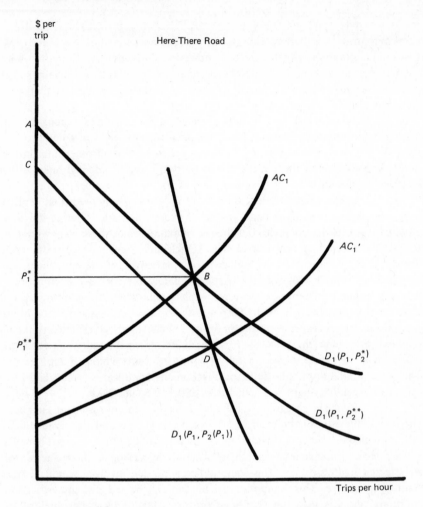

Figure 8-4. Direct and Indirect Effects of Road Improvements with Zero Tolls

say—is charged, OA trips per hour would be taken, this being the travel rate at which the price charged for trips equals the number demanded at that price. With this travel rate, total hourly benefits equal the area $FCBI$—a traveler benefit of FCH plus tolls of $HCBI$.

Consumer benefits with the 1-cent toll exceed by area $GECH$ those associated with a marginal cost price. However, this increase in consumer benefits is more than offset by the associated reduction in highway rents. Specifically, in going from a marginal cost toll to a 1-cent toll, the decrease from GEJ to

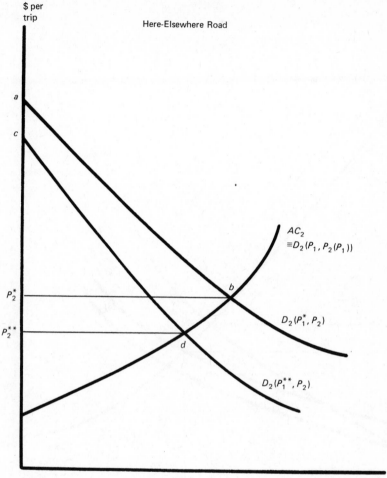

$ per
trip

Here-Elsewhere Road

AC_2
$\equiv D_2(P_1, P_2(P_1))$

a

c

P_2^*

b

$D_2(P_1^*, P_2)$

P_2^{**}

d

$D_2(P_1^{**}, P_2)$

Trips per hour

$HCBI$ in rents collected exceeds the increase, $GECH$, in consumer benefits by an amount equal to area EDC. Put differently, with a 1-cent toll, total short run benefits generated by the highway equal area FEJ minus area EDC.

Area EDC itself can be interpreted as the total short run costs (area $LEDA$) incurred in increasing trip consumption from OL to OA minus the total value (area $LECA$) consumers attach to these additional LA trips. Areas such as EDC are often referred to as "dead-weight losses"—i.e., amounts by which the maximum benefits that could be derived by society from some economic activity are reduced through inefficient pricing.

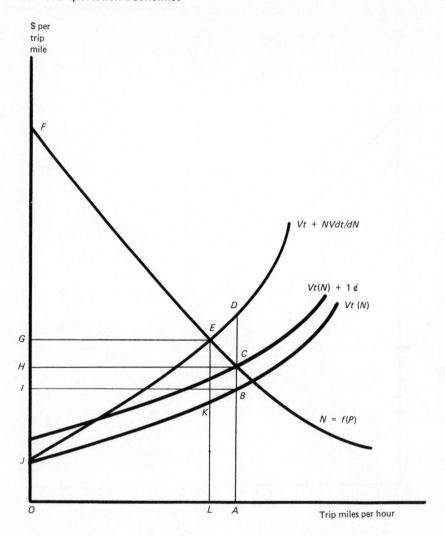

Figure 8-5. Direct Benefits of Road Use with Inefficient Tolls

Suppose that an improvement is made to a highway which is initially priced in the inefficient fashion described in Figure 8-5. As a result, the situation depicted in Figure 8-6 comes about. Even with the improved highway, a 1 cent per mile toll is less than that required to equate demand and marginal cost schedules. A dead-weight loss is therefore still involved in the highway's pricing. However, the size of the loss has diminished from *BCD* to *EFG*. The incremental net benefit of the improvement can therefore be viewed as *ABEH*

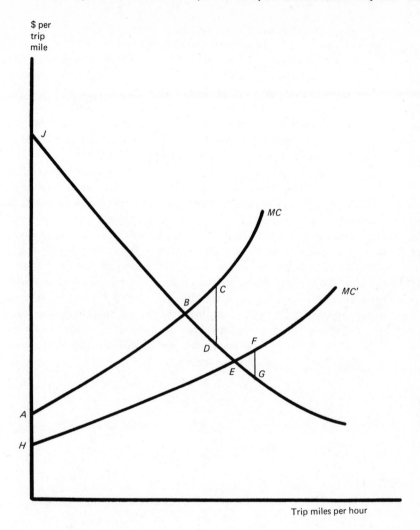

Figure 8-6. Change in Dead-Weight Loss with Road Improvement

(the equivalent of, e.g., *BDEA* in Figure 8-2) *plus* the difference between *BCD* and *EFG*.

To generalize, a given improvement to a highway will lead to a somewhat greater net benefit if its services are initially underpriced than if a marginal cost price is charged for them. By the same token, however, a given improvement will lead to a smaller net benefit if a highway's services are initially overpriced rather than priced at marginal cost. That is, if price initially exceeds marginal cost, an improvement will almost invariably serve to increase the gap between price and marginal cost thereby increasing the deadweight loss.

At least on urban highways, the user charge implicit in gasoline and related excises seems typically to fall considerably short of the appropriate marginal cost toll during peak travel periods and to be somewhat greater than marginal cost during other times of day. This being the case, the changes in deadweight losses associated with urban highway improvements tend to offset each other. An improvement can generally be expected to decrease deadweight losses during peak travel hours but to increase them during off-peak hours.

To summarize, if marginal cost tolls are levied on highway networks, estimating the total benefits to society that would result from an improvement require only data on the use made of that improvement. This is true even though the improvement can be expected to alter traffic conditions on other parts of the highway network and (see Chapters Ten and Eleven) change other prices in the economy. If failure to price at marginal cost is pervasive in the network, however, improving one of its links may change the dead-weight losses associated with other links. To the degree that it does, complete estimation of the improvement's benefits requires estimation of the changes to which it gives rise in deadweight losses throughout the system. Again, however, it is only changes in deadweight losses that must be estimated on those portions of the network that are not directly involved in the improvement, not the benefits to consumers associated with changes in trip prices on these segments.

Chapter Nine

Consumers' Surplus versus National Income Change Benefit Measures

The benefits a society derives from a dam, a road, or any other asset can, as Chapter Eight suggests, be regarded as the sum of the consumers' surplus and the quasi-rents resulting from use of the asset. The aggregate benefits afforded by *all* the assets at the society's disposal could, in principle, be measured by carefully[a] adding up the surpluses and rents associated with their use. Enormous data problems would be involved in constructing such an aggregate measure, of course. If only for this reason, no one has seriously undertaken the task.

Quantitative comparisons of the aggregate well-being of an individual country at different points in time or of different countries at the same point in time are almost invariably based on one or another statistic derived from national income accounts. A country's national product can be defined roughly[b] as the sum of the market values of the goods and services purchased by its business firms for investment purposes, by its households for consumption, and by its government agencies. Associated with each dollar's worth of national product is a dollar's worth of payments to primary factors of production—land, labor, and capital. A country's national income is the sum of these factor payments.[c]

Just as total consumers' surplus plus rents could, at least in principle, be substituted for national income or national product as a measure of aggre-

---

[a]The consumers' surplus associated with the output of a flour mill derives from the demand for the bread produced by the bakeries that the flour mill supplies. Simple addition of the bread and flour consumers' surpluses would therefore entail counting the same benefit twice. Care would have to be taken to avoid this sort of double counting in adding up the benefits from individual assets to arrive at a societywide aggregate.

[b]This is hardly a place for a detailed exposition of national income accounting principles. For such an exposition, see, e.g., Samuelson [4], ch. 10.

[c]This definition ignores the existence of indirect business taxes. The market price of a package of cigarettes—its contribution to national product under the usual definition—involves the state and federal excise taxes that are imposed on it. The factor payments to which it gives rise—its contribution to national income—is less than its contribution to national product by the amount of these taxes.

gate well-being, the contribution to national income or national product of an investment project could be substituted for the consumers' surplus and rents it generates as a measure of its benefits. Indeed, several recent studies (see, for example, Bos and Koyck [1], Brown and Harral [2], Friedlaender [3], and Tinbergen [5]) have proposed just this sort of evaluative framework for transportation investment projects. Those studies that carried out actual numerical calculations found the "change in national income" benefit measure to be larger—typically by a substantial amount—than that yielded by the "traditional [consumers' surplus] appraisal scheme."[d] The writers involved typically attributed this difference to failure of the traditional scheme to account for the indirect benefits of transportation improvements.

These findings raise several questions: What is the relationship between the consumers' surplus measure of an investment project's benefits and the project's effect on national income? Do transportation improvements always lead to greater increases in national income than in consumers' surplus? Are transportation improvements unique in this regard? Or would the same qualitative findings apply to any other investment project?

Considering a very simple but, in many underdeveloped areas quite realistic, economic system will prove helpful in answering these questions. Those who live in many isolated villages in the tropical rain forest area of West Africa survive by raising a few basic subsistence crops—yams, cassava, field rice, or plantain, as the case may be. In addition, they produce for sale either a surplus of their subsistence crops or coffee, cocoa, oil palm kernels, or some other agricultural commodity. At irregular intervals, one of these bush dwellers loads 50 or so pounds of these crops on his head and carries them along a jungle trail to a market town at some distance from his village. There he sells his produce, uses the proceeds to buy a few basic imported commodities—salt, tobacco, cloth, Coca-Cola—and head loads these purchases back to his village.

Suppose (1) that a representative bush dweller restricts his market dealings to transactions in palm kernels and cloth, (2) that the prices of these commodities (determined is competitive world markets that are unaffected by either his transactions or those of this country) are P_k and P_c per pound and per yard respectively, (3) that it takes him X hours to produce 50 pounds of palm kernels, Y hours to carry them to market, and an additional Y hours to make the back haul journey with the cloth he buys, and (4) that he regards head loading and producing palm kernels as being equally onerous activities.

Under these circumstances, it seems reasonable to regard his hourly money wage rate, W, as being equal to $50 P_k/(X + Y)$—his receipts from selling 50 pounds of kernels divided by the number of hours required to produce and transport them to market. If he makes K such trips a year, the annual contribution of his palm kernel production and transportation activities to national

[d]The terminology is that of Bos and Koyck [1].

product is 50 $P_k K$ while his contribution to national income is $W(X + Y)K$. The dollar values of these two contributions are, of course, the same. In addition, it seems reasonable to add a contribution of WYK—his wage rate times the total number of hours he spends on return trips from the market—to cover the value he adds to his cloth by carrying it back to his village from the market town.[e] For simplicity, the contributions of his subsistence farming activities to national income and national product will be ignored in what follows.

Suppose, for the sake of still further specificity, that X and Y respectively equal 30 hours and 10 hours, that P_c equals $1 per yard and P_k equal 5 cents per pound and that, at these prices, the bush dweller chooses to make one round trip to market each week. With the proceeds of this trip, he buys 2½ yards of cloth. His annual contribution to national product would be 5¢ per lb. X 50 lb. per wk. X 52 wk. per yr. = $130 per yr. for his palm kernel marketing activities plus an additional $32.50 for the value he adds to cloth by transporting it back to his village. His hourly wage rate would be 6.250 cents.

This equilibrium underlies A in Figure 9-1. At this point, the line *EA* is tangent to the curve *FAG*. *EA* shows the alternative combinations of yards of cloth on the one hand and, on the other, hours devoted to "leisure"—more exactly, leisure and subsistence farming activities—that the bush dweller could obtain with the 168 hours in a week. The line *FAG* is one of his leisure-cloth indifference curves. It shows alternative combinations of leisure and cloth that would leave the bush dweller feeling equally well off. Point A, then, indicates that combination of these commodities at which the bush dweller would maximize his utility given the constraint on his ability to trade leisure for cloth that is imposed by market forces and the available technology.

Suppose, now, that the bush dweller discovers a new trail that cuts the time require for a round trip to market from 20 to 10 hours. As a result, his real wage—the rate at which he can trade leisure for cloth—increases. Specifically, the technology-market constraint that he faces shifts from *EA* to *EFG* in Figure 9-1. Knowledge about the position of another leisure-cloth indifference curve would be required to specify the point on this new constraint that will maximize his utility. In the absence of this information, about all that can be said is that the new tangency between an indifference curve and the technology-resources constraint will not lie to the northwest of F or to the southeast of G. Tangencies in these regions would involve indifference curves that cross—a

---

[e]The bush dweller produces trips to and from market in rigidly fixed proportions. A cost allocation problem of the sort discussed in Chapter Six therefore arises in dividing the cost of a round trip into a portion attributable to hauling kernels to market and another to bringing cloth back to the village. Had these costs been allocated on other than a 50-50 basis, the formula for determining the real wage rate imputed to the bush dweller as well as that for his contribution to national income would have differed from those given in the text. However, the conclusions reached below would not be altered in any essential way.

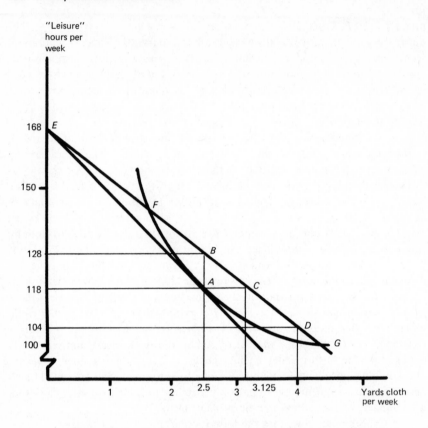

Figure 9-1. Bush Dweller's Alternative Responses to Discovery of New Path

situation inconsistent with the assumption that he strives to maximize his utility. A tangency anywhere on the line segment *FG* is, however, consistent with utility maximization.

The implications, of alternative tangencies at *B, C,* and *D* are particularly worth exploring. Suppose, first, that the bush dweller winds up at *B*. At this point, he continues to consume 2½ yards of cloth a week. He does so, however, at a cost of 40 rather than 50 hours a week spent processing palm kernels and transportation. At *B* he is, in effect, using all the gain in his real wage rate to buy increased leisure. At *C* in Figure 9-1 the bush dweller uses all his real wage increase to increase his cloth consumption. He continues to spend 50 hours a week on gathering and transportation activities. During the average week, this effort involves his collecting 62.5 pounds of kernels, completing 1¼ round trips to market, and increasing his cloth consumption from 2½ to 3⅛ yards. Finally, at point *D*, the bush dweller responds to his increased real wage by increasing the number of hours he participates in the market economy. Specifically, he sacrifices 64 hours of leisure each week to acquire 4 yards of cloth.

Points *B, C,* and *D* involve different contributions by the bush dwellers's market activities to national income and national product. Computing these changes is quite straightforward. To repeat, the annual contributions of these activities to national income was calculated as $130, attributable to the palm kernels he delivered to market, plus an additional $32.50 to reflect the value he added to cloth by transporting it back to his village. The total of these two contributions works out to the equivalent of $3.125 a week. Point *B* involves no increase in cloth consumption, palm kernel production, or trips to market. As a result, the bush dweller's contribution to national income is the same at point *B* as at point *A*. Points *C* and *D* involve increases in both palm kernel output and trips to market of, respectively, 25 and 60 percent. If the wage rates and prices which prevailed prior to discovery of the new trail are used to value these increases in output,[f] they involve respective increases in the bush dweller's weekly contribution to national income of 0.25 × $3.125 = $0.78125 and 0.60 × $3.125 = $1.875.

Computing the consumers' surplus measure of the benefit to the bush dweller resulting from his discovery of the new trail requires a bit of additional calculation. If his prediscovery hourly wage rate can be regarded as 6.25 cents per hour, then the money equivalent of a 20-hour round trip is $1.25 (= 20 hours per trip × 6.25 cents per hour). Still valuing the bush dweller's time at 6.25 cents an hour, the new path reduces this money equivalent to 62.5 cents. In the absence of information on his responses to trip costs between $0.625 and $1.25, and exact picture of his alternative demand schedules for trips cannot be sketched. However, the true demand relationships associated with points *B, C,* and *D* respectively in Figure 9-1 would probably not differ significantly from the straight lines *HJ, HK,* and *HL* drawn in Figure 9-2.

Although the *HJ* demand schedule shows no change in the number of trips taken as a result of the decrease in the price of trips, it still involves a consumers' surplus benefit equal to the vertically shaded area. The numerical value of this areas is

$$1 \text{ trip per week} \times (\$1.25 \text{ per trip} - \$0.625 \text{ per trip}) = \$0.625 \text{ per week}$$

In addition to the vertically shaded area, the *HK* demand schedule involves a benefit (the horizontally shaded area in Figure 9-2) attributable to the additional one-quarter trip per week that the bush dweller would take at point *C* in Figure 9-1. This additional benefit equals approximately 7.8 cents per week.

---

[f]This is the valuation procedure employed in the studies mentioned above which proposed national income measures of transportation improvement benefits.

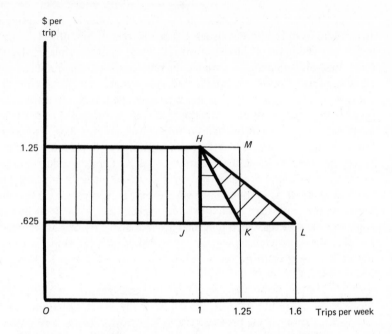

Figure 9-2. Changes in Consumers' Surplus and National Income with Discovery of New Path

Finally, the *HL* demand schedule involves a benefit of 37.5 cents (the horizontally plus the diagonally shaded area in Figure 9-2) in addition to the benefit on the one trip per week that was taken at a price of $1.25 a trip. In summary, the weekly benefits attributed to the new path by the national income and consumers' surplus measurement techniques at points *B, C,* and *D* respectively are:

	B	*C*	*D*
National income increase	–	78.1¢	$1.875
Consumers' surplus increase	62.5¢	70.3¢	$1.000

The first point worth noting about this comparison is that the increase in national income resulting from a transportation improvement need not be greater than the consumers' surplus benefit measure associated with that improvement. In particular, at point *B,* the consumers' surplus measure shows a gain despite the fact that national income does not change. More generally, the less elastic is the demand for trips the more likely it is that the consumers' surplus benefit measure will exceed the national income change measure.

The cause of the differences between these two benefit measures can be stated quite simply: national income and consumers' surplus do not measure the same thing. There is therefore no reason to suppose that any alteration in an economy that leads to a change in national income will lead to a change of equal magnitude in consumers' surplus. In Figure 9-3, when the price of widgets is *OB*, their contribution to national income (equals national product) is the rectangle *OBCD* and the consumers' surplus generated by them is the triangle *ABC*. If an improvement in technology leads to a decline in their price, then consumers' surplus increases by *BCGJ* while national income evaluated at preimprovement prices increases by *DCFH*. While circumstances exist in which these two magnitudes would be equal, it seems clear that these circumstances could not be expected to prevail universally.

To elaborate: Computing national income involves adding up the receipts of primary factors of production—land, labor, and capital—that result from market transactions. In comparing the national incomes of two time periods, the prices used in weighting individual transactions are sometimes those of the individual time periods. It is more common, however, to adjust for such changes in prices as may occur by using a single set of prices to weight trans-

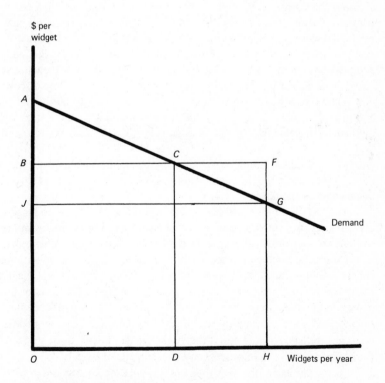

Figure 9-3. Comparison of National Income and Consumers' Surplus Benefit Measures

actions in both time periods. Thus, in the case currently under examination, the prices in effect before discovery of the new path are used to weight both pre- and postdiscovery transations.

In computing national income or national product, no account is taken of the fact that people enjoy leisure as well as what they can buy with the cash they receive from working or from selling the services of assets they own. Similarly, no account is taken of the fact that the utility an individual derives from consuming an additional unit of a commodity decreases with increases in the number of units he consumes. These facts *are* taken into account in computing consumers' surplus measures, however, and they are of particular relevance in comparing the consumers' surplus and national income change measures associated with point *C* in Figure 9-1. To repeat, at this point the bush dweller devotes the same number of hours (50 a week) to market related activities before and after his discovery of the new path. His leisure hours remain unchanged. Hence, none of the difference between the two measures can be attributed to differences in their treatments of leisure.

In determining the benefits the bush dweller derives from additional trips, the consumers' surplus calculations have the effect of assigning these trips a price of $(1.25 + 0.625)/2$—a value midway between the new and old prices. However, in valuing the additional output with which these trips are associated (additional palm kernels delivered to market and value added to the additional yards of cloth that are transported to the village), the national income calculations assign prices equal to those which prevailed before discovery of the new path. Had a prediscovery price also been assigned to additional trips in the consumers' surplus calculations, the benefit inputed to these trips would have doubled. The rectangle *HJKM* in Figure 9-2 has an area of 15.6 cents, while that of the horizontally shaded triangle *HJK* is 7.8 cents. Having made this change in the price used for valuation, consumers' surplus calculations would have yielded precisely the same benefit—78.1 cents per week—as the national income change calculations.

This finding can be generalized. *If* a change takes place which increases the output obtainable from a given set of primary resources, and *if* the primary resources allocated to market activities do not themselves change, and *if* the same pricing rules are used in consumers' surplus as in national income change benefit calculations, then both calculation schemes will yield the same numerical result. Thus, the fact that point *D* in Figure 9-1 is associated with a higher national income than consumers' surplus benefit reflects the different pricing rules that are employed and the fact that the national income measure does not reflect the disutility the bush dweller incurs from using what were formerly leisure hours to process and transport palm kernels.

Similarly, the fact that the national income measure is less than the consumers' surplus measure at point *B* reflects the fact that the national income measure takes no credit for the additional utility the bush dweller derives from increasing his leisure activities. As it happens, a positively sloped supply schedule—i.e., a positive relationship between the real wages of primary factors of production and the rates at which their services are offered for sale—was assumed in all the studies mentioned above in which numerical calculations revealed national income changes to be greater than changes in benefits as traditionally measured.

The conclusions that have been reached in this chapter are by no means restricted to transportation improvements. The specific change in the bush dweller's economic environment that led him to shift from an equilibrium at *A* in Figure 9-1 to one at *B*, *C*, or *D* was his discovery of a new path. However, any change in the environment that shifts the technology-market constraint facing him from *EA* to *EFG* would have precisely the same effect. From his point of view, equivalent changes include discovery of a new picking or processing technology or a new stand of palm trees that reduce by 10 hours the time required to prepare 50 pounds of palm kernels for market, an increase in the world market price of palm kernels from 5 cents to 6.25 cents per pound, and a decrease in the market price of cloth from $1 to 80 cents a yard.

Thus, if an economic environment is such that a transportation improvement would lead to a substantially greater increase in the national income than in the consumers' surplus measure of its benefits, any other favorable change in the environment would likely yield the same result. The primary source of discrepancies between benefits as measured by these two techniques is a state of affairs in which supplies of primary factors are positively (or negatively) related to the real earnings rates of these factors. Such discrepancies do not depend on the peculiar virtues of transportation, or of any other type of public investment.

Chapter Ten

Transportation Improvements and Land Values

Many studies have demonstrated that land values tend to increase—often dramatically—in the vicinity of newly improved highways. Since these increases are independent of the highway use of the affected property owners, their gains are quite properly labeled "nonuser benefits." Should these gains be regarded as benefits over and above those that accrue to highway users? That is, should they be regarded as benefits that must in some way be added to those arising directly from highway use if total highway benefits are to be estimated accurately?[a]

As an aid in answering these questions, it is useful to explore the impact of a transportation improvement on a hypothetical economy having the following characteristics.[b] A city (conceived, for simplicity, as a single point) is located in the center of an undifferentiated, uniformly fertile plain. Land on the plain is useless except to produce food for sale in the city. Food production is a fixed coefficients (i.e., Type II) process—that is, when combined with one square mile of land, resources with a market values of C will produce one unit of food. The use of more than C worth of resources on a square mile will yield no additional output; if resources equal to, say, 50 percent of C are applied to a square mile, output of one-half a unit of food will result. Transportation can take place in a straight line in any direction. The cost of shipping a unit of food one mile is initially t.

In this economy, someone would find it worthwhile to farm any land for which food production costs are less than the net return or FOB price of food at his farm—the difference between its market price and the cost of

---

[a]U.S. Bureau of Public Roads [5] both gives an emphatic "yes" answer to these questions (p. 78) and provides summaries of a considerable number of studies of the relationship between highway improvements and land value changes (pp. 5-25, 54-60).

[b]In Mohring [2] (pp. 236-244), I explored the ramifications of a similar model, as did Walters [4] (ch. 5). The antecedents of both models are to be found in studies by Ellet [1] and von Thunen [3] in the early nineteenth century.

transporting it from the farm to the city. At a farm D miles from the city, the FOB price of a unit of food is $P - Dt$, where P is the market price of food. Let $D*$ denote the distance between the city and the cultivated land farthest from it. The FOB price of food grown on this land will just suffice to cover production costs. That is,

$$P - D*t = C \quad \text{or} \quad D* = (P - C)/t.$$

Since travel can take place in a straight line in any direction, the cultivated area will take the form of a circle of radius $D*$ miles centered on the city. If one square mile of land produces one unit of food, both the area of the cultivated zone and the food output that would be induced by a market price of P can be written as $\Pi(D*)^2$. Thus,

$$Q = \Pi(D*)^2 = K[(P - C)/t]^2$$

is the food supply schedule—the amount of food that would be grown for transportation to the city at alternative market prices. This supply schedule is plotted as the line CS in Figure 10-1.

Both $D*$ and the actual price of food in the city will be determined by the intersection of this supply schedule with the food demand schedule (the line DD in Figure 10-1) of city residents. If these two schedules intersect at point A, OF units of food will be produced at a market price of OP per unit. The total expenditures on food by city residents will then equal the area $OPAF$. Of this total outlay, an amount equal to the area $OCBF$ will go to pay for the resources directly employed in food production. An amount equal to ABC will be paid for the resources used in transporting food to the city. Finally, revenues equal to the area PAC will accrue as rents to the owners of farm land at a distance of less than $D*$ miles from the city.

The sources of these rents can perhaps be made more clear by referring to Figure 10-2. It shows the relationship between FOB price and distance along a straight line extending from the city to the boundary of the cultivated zone. The price paid in the city for a unit of food is independent of the distance from the city at which it is grown. However, the FOB price at a farm declines steadily with distance from the city untill, at a distance of $D*$, the net return just suffices to cover production costs.

For farms that are closer to the city than $D*$, something is left over after transportation and production costs have been paid. This "something" accrues as rents to the owners of land which is more productive than that at the boundary of the agricultural zone. Nearby land is *not* more productive in the sense of yielding a greater food output per square mile with a given quantity of resources. (By assumption, all land is of equal fertility.) Rather, close-in land

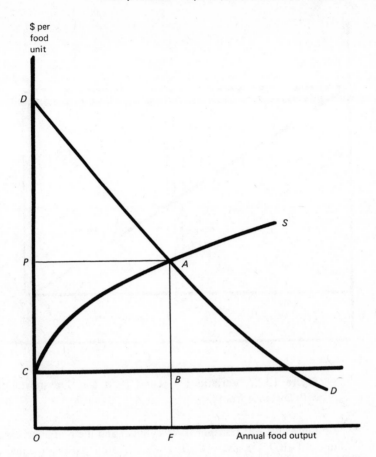

Figure 10-1. Food Supply and Demand Relationships with Costly Transportation

is more productive in that it yields a given quantity of food *delivered at the city,* with a lower total expenditure on both production and transportation.

The total food expenditures of city residents can be visualized as equal to the volume generated by rotating the rectangle $OPSD^*$ around the line OP extending upward from the city. The result of this rotation is a cylinder with a base of $\Pi(D^*)^2$, a height of P, and hence a volume of $P \cdot \Pi(D^*)^2$. This large cylinder can be viewed as comprised of three parts: food production costs, a cylinder with a height of C and hence a volume of $C \cdot \Pi(D^*)^2$; total rents, a cone with a height of $P - C$ and a volume of $(P - C) \cdot \Pi(D^*)^2/3$; and transportation costs, what is left of a cylinder with a height of $(P - C) = D^*t$ after the rent cone has been subtracted out.

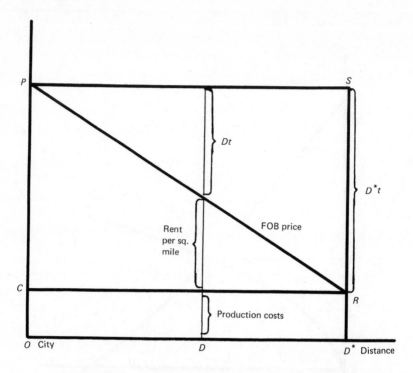

Figure 10-2. Variations in Land Rent and Transportation Costs with Distance from City

Since the rent-transport cost cylinder and the rent cone have respective volumes of $\Pi(D^*)^3 t$ and $(1/3)\Pi(D^*)^3 t$, transport costs are equal to $(2/3)$ $\Pi(D^*)^3 t$. Thus the area ABC under the supply schedule in Figure 10-1, which equals the costs of transporting OF units of food per year to the city, is precisely twice the area PAC, which equals the annual rents that accrue to the owners of close-in farm land.

Suppose, now, that a costless innovation is made in transportation technology that reduces the per-mile costs of transporting a unit of food from t to βt. Suppose also that the demand by city residents for food is totally inelastic—that the same quantity of food will be consumed regardless of the market price. This improvement will reduce the cost of shipping a unit of food to the city from land at the boundary of the agricultural zone from $D^* t$ to $\beta D^* t$. The improvement will also serve to reduce the total costs incurred in transporting OF units of food to the city by an amount equal to $(1 - \beta) \cdot (2/3)\Pi$ $(D^*)^3 t$.

Since the innovation would allow resources formerly used in transporting food to be devoted to the satisfaction of other social wants, it would seem highly desirable. Nevertheless, not all members of the population would benefit from the improvement unless the government takes steps to redistribute the gains to which it gives rise. In the absence of redistribution, the improvement would be favored by residents of the city but opposed by the owners of farm land.

To see why this is the case, note that the price of food in the city is determined by the cost of producing food and transporting it to the city from the boundary of the agricultural zone. Since this cost had declined by $(1 - \beta)$ D^*t, so too will the price of food. Thus, total expenditures on food by city residents would decline by $(1 - \beta) \cdot (P - C) \cdot \Pi(D^*)^2 = (1 - \beta) \Pi(D^*)^3 t$–an amount 50 percent greater than the underlying reduction in total transportation costs. That benefits to city dwellers exceed the resource savings afforded by the improvement results from the fact that, under the circumstances hypothesized, aggregate land rents are equal to precisely half of aggregate transportation costs. Thus an X change in these costs will be accompanied by a change of precisely $X/2$ in aggregate rents.

Just as with the Here-There road improvement discussed in Chapter Eight, changes in rents resulting from transportation improvement involve transfers of income among population groups. In Chapter Eight, the transfer was between travelers and society at large in the person of the toll collecting agency; in the present example, it is between land owners and the city dwellers who consume food. These income transfers involve gains to those whose incomes increase that are, in a purely financial sense, exactly offset by losses to those whose incomes decrease. To the extent that society regards those who gain as being more deserving than those who lose, these financial transfers involve net benefits. However, if society accepts the compensation principle or, less generally, regards rent receivers and rent payers as equally deserving, transfers of income between these two groups cancel out in a welfare as well as a financial sense.

It should be emphasized that the basic aim of the preceding pages has been to demonstrate that such changes in land values as may result from transportation improvements involve transfers of income among members of the population, not additional benefits (or losses) that must in some fashion be added to those arising directly from the improvement. These pages were not intended to show that transportation improvements inevitably make land owners worse off. A different transportation improvement or a higher elasticity of demand for food[c] would lead it to be in the selfish interests of at least some landlords to support transportation improvements.

As for changing the assumed nature of the transportation improvement: Suppose that a straight, unlimited access, express road is built west from the city into its agricultural hinterland; that the cost of shipping food a mile along this road is a fraction, a, of the value prevailing in the remainder of the economy; and that a is unaffected by the amount of traffic on the road. Contin-

[c]That is, a greater percentage change in the quantity of food demanded as a result of a given percentage change in its price.

ue to assume that the demand for food in the city is totally inelastic. Those who farm the land adjacent to the new road will, of course, use it to ship their output to the city. In addition, those who farm in a region near but not immediately adjacent to the road (the "impact zone") will find that they can reduce their transportation costs by using a somewhat circuitous route.

For example, instead of shipping directly to the city, a farmer located at (X_1, Y_1) in Figure 10-3 will take his food to some point $(X_o, 0)$ on the road and then use it for the remainder of each shipment to the city. By taking this circuitous route, his total cost of transporting a unit of food is

$$T = X_o \, a \, t + [Y_1^2 + (X_o - X_1)^2]^{\frac{1}{2}} t.$$

The first term on the right of this expression is the cost of shipping a unit of food X_o miles along the highway. The second is t times the distance between (X_1, Y_1) and $(X_o, 0)$. It can be shown[d] that this total cost would be a minimum if the farmer selects the point, X_o, at which his shipments enter the highway to satisfy

$$X_o = X_1 - a \, Y_1/(1 - a^2)^{\frac{1}{2}}$$

This is the heavy line in Figure 10-3 connecting $(X_o, 0)$ with (X_1, Y_1).

This specific circuitous route would be followed not only by the farmer at (X_1, Y_1) but also by every other farmer located along the line terminating at X_o. These same considerations apply to each of the additional lines drawn in Figure 10-3. That is, all impact zone farmers located along any line of the form

$$X = A + aY/(1 - a^2)^{\frac{1}{2}} \quad \text{or} \quad X = A - aY/(1 - a^2)^{\frac{1}{2}}$$

will ship their food to the same point on the artery. The impact zone will be bounded by those values of X and Y for which $A = 0$, i.e., by the lines

$$X = aY/(1 - a^2)^{\frac{1}{2}} \quad \text{and} \quad X = - aY/(1 - a^2)^{\frac{1}{2}}$$

The existence of the artery will not just affect the shipping patterns of those who farm near it. It will also alter the spatial configuration of the cultivated zone. Consider, for example, a farmer initially located at the point $(0, D^*)$ in Figure 10-3—that is, due north of the city at the boundary of the cultivated zone that had been established before construction of the new road. If

---

[d]By differentiating T with respect to X_o, setting the resulting expression equal to zero, and rearranging terms.

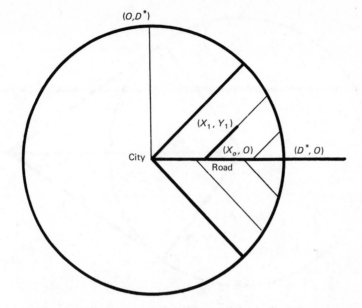

Figure 10-3. Effect of Road Improvement on Travel Patterns

land values remained unchanged, this farmer could move from free (i.e., zero rent) land at his original location to free land at (D^*, O). By doing so, he would reduce the cost of shipping a unit of his output to the city from D^*t to αD^*t.

Market forces can be expected to work toward minimizing the costs of transporting the fixed quantity of food demanded in the city. As a result, the cultivated zone would expand at the periphery of the impact zone and contract at the periphery of the nonimpact zone. Ultimately, a new equilibrium pattern of land use of the sort depicted in Figure 10-4 will be established. In this equilibrium, the total area devoted to farming will be the same as before construction of the new road. As a result, the cost of transporting a unit of food to the city from anywhere on the boundary of the cultivated zone will have declined from D^*t to $D't$.

By arguing along precisely the same lines as were used in discussing a uniform reduction in transportation costs, it can be demonstrated that the aggregate cost reduction afforded by the new road will be

$$(1 - D'/D^*) \cdot (2/3) \cdot \Pi(D^*)^3 t$$

As in the case of the simpler improvement, constructing the highway will reduce aggregate land rents by precisely half this amount. This reduction in land values will be distributed over space differently than was the case with the simple im-

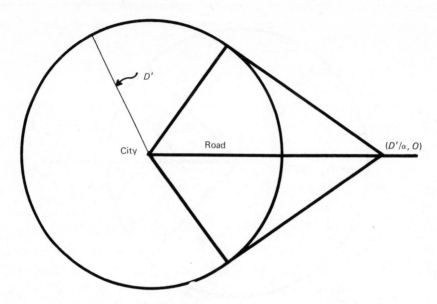

Figure 10-4. Effect of Road Improvement on Land Use

provement. Any square mile that continues to be cultivated in the nonimpact zone will suffer the same reduction in rent, regardless of its distance from the city. Specifically, this reduction will be $(D^* - D')t$. Hence, aggregate expenditures on food will decline by $(1 - D'/D^*) \cdot \Pi(D^*)^3 t$—an amount 50 percent greater than the aggregate reduction in transportation costs. The aggregate of rents received by landlords in the nonimpact zone and close to the boundary of the impact zone will decline by somewhat more than the difference between the changes in transportation costs and food expenditures. Rents in most of the impact zone will increase, however.

While the redistribution of income brought about the construction of the highway is somewhat more complicated than that involved in a uniform reduction in transportation costs, the essential conclusion of the earlier analysis remains unchanged. Unless those who gain (city dwellers and some impact area landlords) are deemed more (or less) deserving than those who lose, the reduction in aggregate land rents cannot be regarded as a benefit or a loss to the community at large.

If the assumption is dropped that food consumption is independent of the price of food, the relation between land values and transport costs cannot be specified without further information even in the simple economy under discussion. Rather, the effect on land values of transportation improvements will depend on both the relative importance of transportation costs in the delivered price of food and the elasticity of demand for food. If both magnitudes are substantial, an increase in aggregate land values (but not in the prices of all land parcels) would result from a transportation improvement.

To see why this is the case, suppose that *ABD* in Figure 10-5 is the food demand schedule. Also, suppose once more that a costless improvement in transportation technology takes place that decreases the cost of transporting a unit of food from *t* to *βt* per mile anywhere in the plain surrounding the city. As a result, the food supply schedule shifts from *CAS* to *CBS'* in Figure 10-5. The level of food output which equates supply and demand increases from *OF* to *OF'* and the price of food in the city falls from *OP* to *OP'*.

Although the geometry is slightly different, the benefit implications of this improvement can be discussed in terms almost identical to those used in dealing with Figure 8-2. The benefit to city dwellers afforded by the transportation improvement is area *PABP'*—their increase in consumers' surplus. The benefit to society at large is area *ABC*. The consumer benefit and the net social benefit have area *ABG* in common. The difference between the two benefits equals

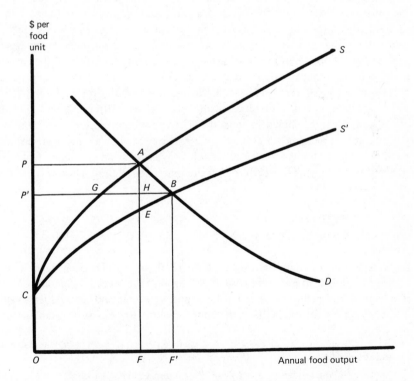

Figure 10-5. Distribution of Transportation Improvement Benefits Between Consumers and Land Owners

PAGP' minus *CBG*. This difference also equals the difference between pre-improvement land rents (area *PAC*) and postimprovement rents (area *P'BC*). If the improvement leaves aggregate rents on farm land unchanged, consumer benefit equals social benefit. If total rents do change, social benefit equals the sum of consumer benefit and the change in land rents.

The effect of the improvement on an individual landlord depends on the proximity of his land to the city. The owner of a farm immediately adjacent to the city would find that his rent per square mile had fallen from *CP* to *CP'* as a result of the improvement. However, someone who owns what was, before the improvement, zero rent land at the boundary of the cultivated zone would now find himself receiving a rent of *HE* per square mile. In general, then, the further away from the city a piece of land is (and hence the greater the absolute reduction in the cost of shipping food from it to the city), the greater is the likelihood that the improvement increases its rent.

To repeat, whether the improvement results in a change in land rents depends on the relative importance of production and shipping costs in the delivered price of food and on the elasticity of demand for it. Letting P equal the price of food, Q equal food output, and C equal the cost of producing a unit of food, the total annual outlays by city dwellers for food equals PQ. Of this total, $(P - C)Q$ goes to cover transportation costs and land rents. Since aggregate transportation costs are twice aggregate land rents regardless of the cost of a unit-mile of transportation services, aggregate rents will increase when transportation costs fall only if $(P - C)Q$ increases when the price of food falls.

Suppose that the demand for food can be written $Q = aP^{-b}$. In this expression, b can be shown to equal the elasticity of demand for food.[e] On substituting this expression for Q in $(P - C)Q$, it can be shown[f] that aggregate expenditures on rent and transportation will increase with a decrease in price only if b is greater than $1/(1 - C/P)$. C/P is the ratio of food production costs to the price of food in the city.

If C/P has a value of:	0.1	0.25	0.5	0.75	0.9
b must be greater than:	1.11	1.33	2.0	4.0	10.0

for a reduction in transportation costs to result in an increase in land rents.

But, just as was the case in dealing with the preceding variants of the simple economy being considered, what happens to total land values is irrelevant in specifying the total benefits of the improvement.[g] Regardless of what changes

---

[e]The elasticity of demand can be written $E = - (dQ/dP) \cdot (P/Q)$ or, for this demand equation, $E = - (abP^{-b-1}) (P/aP^{-b}) = b$.

[f]By differentiating $(P - C) \cdot aP^{-b}$ with respect to P.

[g]Again assuming that society places the same value on the welfare of landlords as on that of city dwellers.

in aggregate land values may occur, the basic benefit of the improvement is the area *ABC* in Figure 10-5. If the elasticity of demand for food is high, and production costs account for a small share of the delivered price of food, most of the benefits of the improvement will be reaped by the owners of distant farm land. If the demand elasticity is small, and production costs bulk large in the delivered price of food, city dwellers will gain more than the total social benefit while landlords as a group will lose. Regardless of how benefits are distributed between city dwellers and landlords as a group, however, those who own the best land— that closest to the city—will be the most likely to incur losses as a result of the improvement.

Chapter Eleven

The "Industrial Reorganization" Benefits of Transportation Improvements

The ability of a firm to exploit manufacturing scale economies can be limited by the cost of transporting its products to market. A reduction in unit transportation costs can therefore yield two types of benefits. First, it provides "direct" benefits by reducing the costs of distributing the outputs of existing manufacturing facilities. Second, a transport cost reduction makes it efficient to expand the outputs and marketing areas of individual production facilities, thereby taking greater advantage of manufacturing scale economies. This use of more transportation-intensive means of production and distribution in response to reduced transportation costs generates "reorganization" benefits.

The twofold impact of transportation improvements has long been recognized. Consider, for example:

> The division of labor. . .must always be limited. . .by the extent of the market. When the market is very small, no person can have any encouragement to dedicate himself entirely to one employment. . . . [B]y means of water carriage a more extensive market is opened to every sort of industry than what land carriage alone can afford it. . . A broad-wheeled waggon, attended by two men, and drawn by eight horses, in about six weeks time carries and brings back between London and Edinburgh near four ton weight of goods. In about the same time, a ship navigated by six or eight good men, and saling between the ports of London and Leith, frequently carries and brings back two hundred ton weight of goods. . . .Were there no other communication between these two places, therefore but by land carriage, . . .they could carry on but a small part of that commerce which at present subsists between them, and consequently give but a small part of that encouragement which they at present mutually afford to each other's industry (Smith [4], pp. 17–19).

Do the analytical frameworks for dealing with transportation improvements that were described in Chapter Eight take into account these "industrial reorganization" benefits of which Adam Smith wrote?[a] Or does adequately accounting for them require the development of special benefit measurement techniques? To see why the answers to these questions are respectively "yes" and "no," it is useful to consider a business firm which has a monopoly over the production of widgets, a commodity it distributes over a wide geographical area.[b] Government regulations require that whatever delivered price it sets must be charged all customers, regardless of transportation costs. At the price charged by the firm, the quantity demanded is the same in each square mile of its market area and equals W_O units per year for the area as a whole.

Inputs are available at prices that are independent of both the locations and outputs of individual widget factories. The manufacturing process entails increasing returns—a doubling of manufacturing inputs at an individual factory would more than double outputs. The output of a given plant can be expanded, however, only by increasing the plant's market area and thus the average cost of transporting widgets to the final consumer. Given these assumptions, the manufacturer would minimize total costs by determining the output per plant, say w^*, which minimizes average manufacturing plus distribution costs, and then establishing W_O/w^* factories[c] distributed through his market area at equal intervals.

Figure 11-1 depicts the cost characteristics of a single plant. The curves ADC_1, APC, and ATC_1 refer respectively to average distribution, average production, and average total costs before a transportation improvement is made. As the figure is drawn, average total costs first decline with increases in output. In this range, the increase in unit transportation costs as output increases is more than offset by the decrease in unit manufacturing costs. Beyond output w_1^*, however, declines in unit manufacturing costs as output increases are less than sufficient to offset increases in unit transportation costs.

The level of output, w_1^*, at which the total of unit production and distribution costs would be a minimum for an individual manufacturing facility depends on a number of factors. Of particular importance are the geographical density of demand for the product, the magnitude of scale economies, and the level of transportation costs. Actually, it is conceivable that no point such as w_1^* would exist. If scale economies are substantial and if unit transportation costs are small, the average total cost curve might well decline over a range of outputs sufficient to minimize the firm's total production and distribution costs

---

[a]The U.S. Bureau of Public Roads [5], (p. 78) gave an emphatic "yes" answer to this question: ". . .the restructuring of households, commerce, and industry influenced by highway improvements engenders other advantages to the community-at-large over and above the savings in transportation cost."

[b]The discussion that follows is based on Mohring and Williamson [3], pp. 251-258.

[c]If W_O/w^* is not an integer, each plant clearly cannot be of size w^*. This problem is ignored here though the analysis could be extended to handle it.

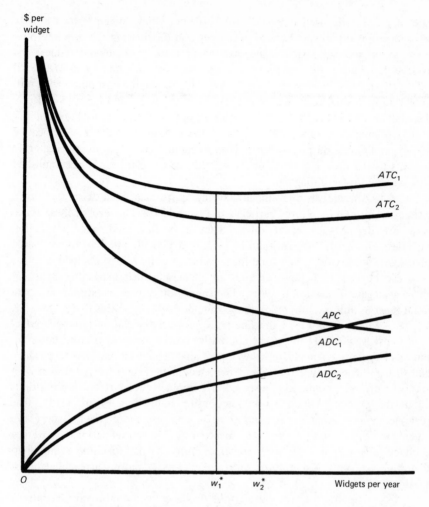

Figure 11-1. Effect of Manufacturing Economies of Scale and Transportation Diseconomies of Scale on Cost Minimizing Output Level

by serving its entire marketing area from a single plant. Under such circumstances, a transportation improvement would not lead the firm to increase its use of transportation services. It would benefit only through reduction in the cost of the transportation it already uses. Since measurement of this benefit is a straightforward matter, attention will be restricted here to cases in which several factories would be required to minimize total production and distribution costs.

A reduction in unit transportation costs would immediately lower the costs of distributing widgets from a group of factories each producing at a rate of w_1^*. In addition, it would make efficient what can be termed a more transportation intensive means of producing and distributing the product. Suppose, to be specific, that a transportation network improvement reduces the average distribution and hence the average total costs of a factory to ADC_2 and ATC_2 respectively. With such a reduction in total costs, the cost minimizing output of an individual plant would increase from w_1^* to w_2^* in Figure 11-1. If the demand for widgets is fixed, this increase in optimum plant size can be realized only by eliminating some production facilities and, at the same time, relocating and expanding the output of others. This being the case, depicting the aggregate benefits to the firm of a transportation improvement can best be accomplished with a second type of diagram.

Alternative total manufacturing costs associated with the firm's given total output are plotted vertically in Figure 11-2a. The level of these aggregate costs depends, to repeat, on the sizes of the firm's individual production facilities. The larger the size (and hence the smaller the number) of individual plants, the lower the firm's total manufacturing costs will be. Individual plant sizes can be increased, however, only by increasing their marketing areas and their aggregate distribution costs. Transportation inputs measured in some homogeneous unit, say ton miles, are plotted horizontally in this figure.

In Figure 11-2a the line $W_o W_o$ is a transportation input–manufacturing cost isoquant. It shows the alternative combinations of transportation inputs and outlays on manufacturing inputs that would be required to produce and distribute W_o widgets to the firm's customers. That $W_o W_o$ is drawn with sort of curvature commonly assumed for isoquants reflects two assumptions about the production-distribution relationship implicit in Figure 11-1. First, scale economies attenuate as plant sizes increase—or, more exactly, successive equal increases in output produce successively smaller reductions in average production costs. Second, the number of units of transportation required to distribute an additional unit of output increases as output at each plant increases.

Suppose that the price (if the firm uses common or contract carriers for distribution) or the cost (if it provides its own distribution services) of transportation services is initially t_1 dollars per ton mile, an amount that is independent of both the length and the size of widget shipments. The straight line $M_1 R_1$ (drawn with a slope of $-t_1$) in Figure 11-2a then represents the alternative combinations of production and transportation inputs that can be purchases with a total budget of OM_1 dollars. Since $M_1 R_1$ is tangent to $W_o W_o$ at R_1, OM_1 is the minimum cost of manufacturing and distributing W_o widgets. At R_1 the firm spends OS_1 on manufacturing inputs and $t_1 \cdot OT_1 = S_1 M_1$ on transportation inputs.

Suppose that improvements are made to the transportation system that reduce the cost of producing ton miles from t_1 to t_2. If the firm provides its own transportation services, it will receive this benefit directly; if it relies

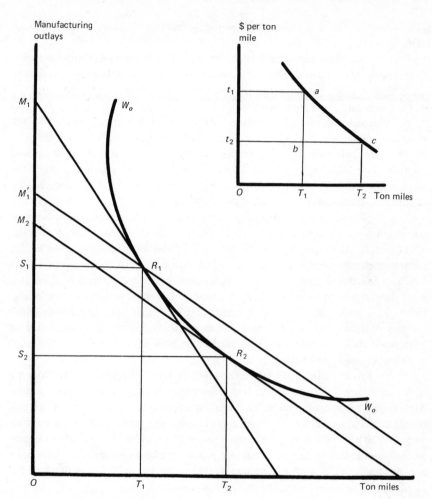

Figure 11-2. Cost Minimizing Choice of Transportation and Manufacturing Outlays

on common or contract carriers and if the transportation industry is competitively organized, it will ultimately receive this benefit through reduced rates. In either event, since a lower outlay is required to purchase a ton mile of transportation services, new and flatter expenditure lines of the sort depicted by $M_1'R_1$ and M_2R_2 become relevant. The former expenditure line shows the benefit to the firm if it continues to produce at point R_1 in Figure 11-2a. At that combination of manufacturing and transportation inputs, the transportation improvement would affect the firm only by reducing the cost of OT_1 ton miles from S_1M_1 to S_1M_1'. This saving can be termed the "direct benefit": the reduction in the cost of the transportation inputs purchased prior to the improvement.

The firm can derive an additional benefit from the improvement. Undertaking the consolidation of production facilities implied by a move to R_2 in Figure 11-2a would entail increasing transportation purchases from OT_1 to OT_2 ton miles and increasing total outlays on transportation from S_1M_1' to S_2M_2. This increase in transportation outlays would be more than offset by the associated reduction of S_1S_2 in the cost of the manufacturing inputs required to produce and distribute W_o widgets. Specifically, the shift from R_1 to R_2 would result in an additional savings of $M_1'M_2$ in total costs. This latter saving is the "reorganization benefit" of the improvement: the cost reduction achievable by substituting transportation for manufacturing inputs.

Figure 11-2b depicts the firm's demand schedule for transportation associated with the shift from R_1 to R_2. In this diagram, the area t_1abt_2 is the direct benefit—the reduction in the cost of OT_1 ton miles brought about by the reduction in their price from t_1 to t_2. This area is equal to M_1M_1' in Figure 11-2a, while the area abc is equal to $M_1'M_2$, the reorganization benefit. That this is the case can most easily be seen by pointing out that, with minor relabeling, Figure 11-2 would describe the behavior of a consumer when faced with simultaneous reductions in his money income and the price of one commodity he buys when these changes leave him indifferent between the new and old sets of price and income (see Hicks [1], ch. 8).

As it shifts along the consumer's W_oW_o indifference curve from R_1 to R_2 in Figure 11-2a, a budget line reflecting these simultaneous price and income adjustments traces out an income compensated or utility constant demand schedule in Figure 11-2b. The area t_1act_2 under this schedule between the new and the old price would exactly equal the reduction in income—M_1M_2 in Figure 11-2a—required to make the consumer indifferent between the new, lower and the old, higher price and income levels—that is, M_1M_2 would exactly equal the I_2-I_1' benefit measure described in Chapter Eight.

As with the consumer, so too with the widget monopolist. Suppose that the transportation improvement only induces him to substitute transportation for manufacturing inputs in the production and distribution of W_o widgets per year. The area t_1act_2 under Figure 11-2b's output-constant demand schedule for transportation inputs would then exactly equal the cost saving which the transportation improvement affords him. If the improvement-induced reduction in outlays for manufacturing inputs, S_1S_2 in Figure 11-2a is treated as an additional benefit, double counting and then some would be involved.

Since the transportation improvement reduces the marginal costs of manufacturing and distributing widgets, it also presumably increases the monopolist's profit maximizing output and decreases his profit maximizing price. If he increases output, his use of additional transportaion inputs would reflect not only substitution effects but also output effects. Even in this case, however, the area under the firm's demand schedule between the new and old prices for transportation services would provide an exact measure of the gain afforded it by the improvement.[d]

Suppose that the firm buys OT ton miles a year at a price of t. This indicates that, when appropriately combined with other inputs, the OT^{th} annual ton mile yields additional revenues (net of outlays on other inputs) of exactly t dollars. Regardless of whether it reflects a fixed or a varying output level, then, the monopolist's derived demand schedule for transportation inputs provides an exact measure of his benefit from a transportation improvement. The measure is the sum over all ton miles used of the difference between the price at which a given ton mile would have been purchased and the price actually paid for that ton mile. To the degree that the transportation improvement leads to a lower price, it also benefits widget consumers. These benefits are not directly reflected in the monopolist's derived demand schedule for transportation inputs.

Suppose the widget industry had been assumed competitively rather than monopolistically organized.[e] Then both the magnitude and the ultimate incidence of the benefits implied by a firm's or the widget industry's derived demand schedule for transportation inputs would be different from those suggested above for monopoly organization. Amplification of these assertions would be called for in a discussion of the benefit implications of changes in the areas under derived demand schedules for different form of market organization.[f]

For the purposes at hand, however, such a discussion is unnecessary. After all, Figure 11-2 can be used to deal with matters other than the utility maximizing allocation of a consumer's budget between one commodity and all others available to him, or with the cost minimizing combination of manufacturing and transportation inputs. With suitable relabeling, the diagrams could also be used to discuss the choices faced by a producer in selecting the cost minimizing quantity of any input used in his production and distribution process. Had "input T" been substituted for "ton miles" or "transportation services" in the above discussion, the conclusions reached would not have changed. A consumers' surplus type measure of transportation improvement benefits would be accurate under precisely the same circumstances as would such a measure of the benefits of any other cost reduction.

[d]This assertion, note, does not hold for what would seem to be the most nearly analogous consumer case: the area under a money income constant demand schedule for a superior good. In this case, as was noted in Chapter Eight, the area under the demand schedule overstates the relevant $I_2 - I_1$ benefit measure.

[e]Since it was the assumed existence of unexploited scale economies at individual manufacturing sites that led to the substitution of transportation for manufacturing inputs in the widget production and distribution process, also to assume the existence of a competitive widget market does involve a contradiction.

[f]This subject is discussed at some length in Mohring and Harwitz [2], pp. 40-56.

This conclusion, it should be noted, is not restricted to a reduction in the cost of an input already employed in a production process. It is equally valid for a cost reduction that leads to the employment of an input which formerly was not used. Indeed, it is valid for input cost reductions that lead entirely new activities to be undertaken. Suppose, for example, that a reduction in the cost of digital computer services leads the widget monopolist to incorporate them into his production process. That the monopolist did not use computers at their old, higher price indicates that their rental rates were greater than the revenues (net of the costs of other inputs) their services would have generated. The benefit he derives from the price reduction is still the sum over all units of computer services purchased of the difference between the price he would have been willing to pay and the price he actually does pay. The only difference between the computer services and the transportation case is that, with computers, benefits are entirely of the "reorganization" variety.

Chapter Twelve

Economies and Diseconomies of Scale in Transportation Activities

Wherever the shape of a cost curve has been of relevance in the preceding chapters of this book, the convenient fiction has been adopted that transportation activities operate under constant returns to scale. That is, it has been assumed that a doubling of outputs requires a doubling of inputs, no more, no less. Actually, scale economies abound in the provision of transportation services, particularly common carrier services. The tasks of this chapter are to spell out general principles of scale economies, to provide specific examples of them in transportation activities, and to quantify these examples where available data permit.

The distinguished British economist, P. Sargant Florence, has classified scale economies (or "principles of efficiency," as he prefers to call them) under three headings: the principles of bulk transactions, multiples, and massed reserves.

The principle of bulk transactions is based on the casual observation that the total money, physical, or psychological costs of dealing with large quantities are sometimes no greater (and usually less than proportionately greater) than those of dealing with small quantities. The amount of work a clerk does in processing an order for 1,000 units is (or at least can be) infinitesimally greater that than involved in an order for one unit. This principle is of particular importance in dealing with common carrier operations. In these operations, for example, an increase in conveyance size requires a less than proportionate increase in crew size. Thus, only one bus or truck driver is needed regardless of the size of the vehicle he operates.

The source of *the principle of multiples* lies in the notion that specialists, be they people or machines, are more efficient producers of goods and services than are generalists. But specialized machines and personnel are indivisible and their capacities may differ. So the problem of balancing capacities arises. To take the common sort of example, suppose that manufacturing widgets requires three separate process units, *A, B,* and *C.* The *A* process has a "natural capacity" of 35 units a day; the *B* process 50 units; and the *C* process 90 units. To produce 90 widgets a day would therefore require one *C* process unit, two *B* units, and three *A* units. At this ouptut level, the *C* unit would be fully employed, but the *B* and *A* units would respectively have 10 and 15 units of unutilized capacity. To minimize the unit costs of producing widgets would require each of the three types of process units to be fully utilized. What output level would be necessary to accomplish this objective? Answering this question requires determining the least common multiple of 35, 50, and 90—the smallest number simultaneously divisible by 35 *and* 50 *and* 90. It turns out to be 3,150.[a]

While 3,150 units per day would be necessary to minimize average costs, increases in daily output would reduce unit costs even at lower production rates. Any output level less than 3,150 per day will involve unutilized capacity in one or more type of process unit. However, unutilized capacity per unit of output will tend to diminish with output increases because only the last process unit(s) added to the widget factory will be less than completely utilized. As output increases, so too does the number of fully employed process units over which the excess capacity of the last machine(s) is averaged in determining unit production costs.

The principle of massed reserves is closely related to the statistician's law of large numbers. In rough terms, this law says that, as the size of the sample drawn from a probability distribution increases, the probability diminishes that the average value of the sample will deviate by, for example, more than 10 percent from the mean of the probability distribution. This law is of relevance wherever the demands for goods or services are subject to uncertainty.

Suppose, for example, that there is a 10 percent chance that a particular type of machine will break down during any given week. A factory would then average ten breakdowns a week if it has 100 such machines, 100 breakdowns a week if it has 1,000 such machines, and so forth. The law of large numbers (or principle of massed reserves) says that the probability that a 1,000-machine factory will experience 120 breakdowns during any given week is less than the probability that a 100-machine factory will experience 12 breakdowns during this week. This means that, *per machine utilized,* the number of spare parts that must be stocked and the number of maintenance personnel that must be hired to achieve any given probability that one or the other will not be available when a breakdown occurs is smaller for the large than for the small factory. As a result, the cost per unit of output of nonroutine maintenance can be expected to diminish with increases in factory size.

---

[a]To rely on grammar school algebra, determining this number requires noting $35 = 7 \times 5$, $50 = 5 \times 5 \times 2$, and $90 = 5 \times 3 \times 3 \times 2$. $7 \times 5 \times 5 \times 3 \times 3 \times 2 = 3,150$ is the smallest number that simultaneously contains all these products of prime numbers and is therefore the smallest number divisible by each of these products.

In what follows, several examples of the principle of bulk transactions as it applies to transportation activities will first be presented. The chapter concludes with examples of situations involving multiples and massed reserve scale economies.

THE "SIX-TENTHS RULE"

Engineering problems exist in supporting the weight of the materials used for coverings of containers. As a result, large containers often require thicker surfaces or more elaborate support structures than do small containers. Still, as a first approximation, the cost of constructing a container can be regarded as approximately proportional to the area of its surface. As an example, the surface area of a spheres is $4\pi R^2$ where R is its radius. Therefore, if cost is proportional to surface area, it can be written as $C = k_1 R^2$ where k_1 is a proportionality constant. The volume of a sphere is $4\pi R^3/3$, a relationship which implies that $R = (3V/4\pi)^{1/3} = k_2 \, V^{1/3}$. Using this relationship to replace R in $C = k_1 R^2$ yields $C = k_1 (k_2 \, V^{1/3})^2 = k_3 \, V^{2/3}$. This expression indicates the cost of the sphere to increase with the two-thirds power of its capacity. Thus, if this relationship holds and if a sphere with a capacity of 100 gallons costs $1,000, then a sphere with a capacity of 200 gallons would cost $1,000 \times 2^{2/3}$ or $1,587. Doubling the container's volume reduces the cost of constructing storage capacity from $1,000 per 100 gallons = $10 per gallon to $1,587 per $2,000 gallons = $7.94 per gallon.

This sort of geometric reasoning plus intensive examination of cost data from facilities of different sizes forms the basis for a rule of thumb that is commonly employed in engineering cost estimation work. Tell a chemical engineer, for example, "This petroleum refinery or sulphuric acid plant will cost $1,000,000 to build." Then ask him, "Please give me a quick judgment as to how much a facility with twice its capacity will cost." He will quite likely work with the equation $C_2 = C_1 (K_2/K_1)^{0.6}$ where C_1 and C_2 reflect the costs of the two facilities and K_1 and K_2 are their respective capacities. Substituting $1,000,000 for C_1 and 2 for K_2/K_1 in this expression yields $1.52 million.

The Pipeline Production Function

A petroleum or natural gas pipeline is basically a long cylinder. Pumps are installed at regular intervals along its length to push a gas or fluid from one point to another. Holding the length and wall thickness of a piece of pipe fixed, the amount of steel it contains is proportional to its circumference, which in turn is proportional to its diameter. This being the case, the cost of constructing one mile of the pipeline cylinder itself is very close to being proportional to its diameter.

Cookenboo [1] reports that an approximate oil pipeline production function can be written as $T = k \, H^{0.4} \, D^{1.7}$ where T is "throughput" (the number of barrels per day transmitted from origin to destination), H is the rate at which horsepower is applied, D is pipeline diameter, and k is a parameter that depends on the distance and terrain traversed by the pipeline and properties (particularly viscosity) of the fluid transmitted. Assuming for simplicity that the costs of pumps and the fuel required to power them is proportional to H,[b] a doubling of expenditures on these inputs would lead to a 4.3-fold increase in throughput.[c] To put it differently, the throughput of a pipeline could be doubled with only a 39 percent increase in expenditures on H and D. Thus, doubling throughput would reduce the cost of transporting a barrel of a specified material by about 30 percent.[d]

Aircraft Operating Costs

An airliner can be viewed as an elaborate container for the movement of people between cities. As such, elements of the six-tenths rule ought to apply to its construction. There are, of course, both physical and conceptual differences between the operations of a gasoline storage tank and an airliner. For one thing, regardless of its size, each passenger aircraft must have exactly one pilot and one copilot. Large aircraft appear to require more pilot and copilot services than do small aircraft. Thus, the top salary paid a pilot of a 350-seat Boeing 747 by one major airline is about $67,000 a year while the same airline pays the pilot of a 100-seat Boeing 727-100 a top salary of only about $42,500 a year. Still, the fact that the number of pilots and copilots is independent of aircraft size introduces a fixed cost into their operation of a sort that leads to the "square root principle" discussed in Chapter Seven and later in this chapter. On the other hand, a number of the costs of providing an airliner's services are more closely related to the capacity of the container than to its surface area. The costs of seats and the salaries of cabin attendants are obvious cases in point.

Analysis of the effect of size on aircraft operating costs is made difficult because small aircraft are generally used for short flights while large aircrafts are used on long flights. Thus, according to the U.S. Civil Aeronautics Board [9], the average stage length (i.e., the average distance covered per aircraft hop in revenue service) of a Boeing 747 and a Douglas DC9 used in domestic service by trunk airlines was 1,962 and 331 miles respectively in 1972. The shorter its stage length, the greater is the fraction of its working day that an aircraft stands waiting at gates, taxiing to and from takeoffs, and climbing to and descending from cruising altitudes.

[b]Actually, large motors both cost less per horsepower than small motors and are somewhat more efficient in their use of fuel. The ensuing calculations therefore understate somewhat the magnitude of pipeline scale economies.

[c]If $T = k \ H^{0.4} \ D^{1.7}$, then $k(2H)^{0.4} \ (2D)^{1.7} = 2^{2.1} \ kH^{0.4} \ D^{1.7} = 4.3T$.

[d]If doubling expenditures on H and D would increase throughput by a factor of $2^{2.1}$, then increasing H and D by a factor of $2^{1/2.1} = 1.39$ would suffice to double throughput. Cost per barrel would then change to $1.39/2 = 0.7$ times their former level.

For this reason, the best available statistic (and even it is less than ideal) for comparing aircraft cost records appears to be cost per block hour.[e] Equations (12-1) and (12-2) report the result of a simple linear regression of an aircraft type's total operating, maintenance, dpreciation, and rental costs per block hour in 1971 and 1972 against the average number of seats it contains. The sample is restricted to those turbo-fan aircraft—thirteen types in 1971, sixteen in 1972—of which ten or more were employed in domestic trunk passenger service during the year in question. Equations (12-3) and (12-4) deal with the same aircraft and years but involve as a dependent variable only operating and maintenance costs.

$$\text{1971 Total Cost} = \$15.58 \times (\text{Seats})^{0.80}$$
$$(R^2 = 0.932) \qquad (12\text{-}1)$$

$$\text{1972 Total Cost} = \$13.38 \times (\text{Seats})^{0.84}$$
$$(R^2 = 0.919) \qquad (12\text{-}2)$$

$$\text{1971 Operating and Maintenance Cost} = \$19.24 \times (\text{Seats})^{0.70}$$
$$(R^2 = 0.916) \qquad (12\text{-}3)$$

$$\text{1972 Operating and Maintenance Cost} = \$17.64 \times (\text{Seats})^{0.73}$$
$$(R^2 = 0.893) \qquad (12\text{-}4)$$

At least four biases that are present in the data underlying these equations should be taken into account in interpreting them. First, while measuring costs on a block hour basis does take into account the time an aircraft spends ascending and descending and taxiing to and from landings and takeoffs, it does not take into account time spent at gates loading, unloading, and being serviced. A number of aircraft operating costs—crew time, in particular—as well as interest on invested capital are more closely related to total time in service than to block hours. An aircraft used for short flights typically provides fewer block hours per day than does one used for long flights. Thus the average Boeing 747 provided 7.87 block hours of service a day in 1972, while the average DC9-10 provided only 5.49.

Offsetting this bias against smaller aircraft to at least some degree are three factors that tend to overstate the costs of large aircraft in equations (12-1)-(12-4). First, the depreciation expenses included in equations (12-1) and (12-2) but excluded from equations (12-3) and (12-4) are based on the initial purchase prices of aircraft, not on their higher replacement costs in pre-

---

[e]The "block-to-block" time of a flight from Here to There is the number of hours that elapse between the time the aircraft first moves under its own power from its gate Here to the time its engines are cut off at its gate There. Cost per block hour is obtained by dividing an aircraft's annual cost by its annual block-to-block hours.

sent day markets. The small planes in the group analyzed tend to be somewhat older than the large ones. Inflation therefore tends to bias the results of equations (12-1) and (12-2) in favor of smaller aircraft.

Leasing practices provide a similar bias. In recent years, airlines have increasingly tended to rent rather than to buy new aircraft. Interest on the capital invested in aircraft is included in the rent lessors collect from airlines but not in the depreciation expenses calculated for airline-owned aircraft. Again, large aircraft tend to be newer than small aircraft.

Still a third bias in favor of small aircraft stems from the responses of several airlines to the disappointing load factors (i.e., ratios of seats occupied to seats available) they experienced when the Boeing 747 was first introduced in late 1969. These airlines attempted to attract more passengers to their jumbo jets by increasing the spaces between seats thereby improving the quality of the service offered. According to the CAB's space standards, a 747 has a seating capacity of 371 if its galley is located on the main passenger deck and 385 if the galley is placed in the cargo area below this deck. In 1971, however, the average 747 flown on domestic trunk routes contained only 328.6 seats. In 1972, this number had declined still further to 317.1. It is the actual average number of seats on an aircraft type, not the CAB's standard number, which enters into equations (12-1) through (12-4).

Unfortunately, the extent to which these and other possible biases in the data underlying the equations offset each other cannot be determined from available information. Still, these equations do rather strongly suggest that economies of aircraft size exist and, indeed, are quite substantial. Balancing as well as is possible the various exponents that appear in the equations and the biases present in the data on which these equations are based, it seems plausible to conjecture that the true costs of an aircraft's services increase with something close to the 0.75 power of its capacity. With this exponent, a doubling of seating capacity would lead to a 68 percent increase in operating costs per block hour and hence to a 16 percent reduction in costs per seat for a flight of any given distance.

SCALE ECONOMIES (AND DISECONOMIES) IN THE GEOMETRY OF TRANSPORTATION RIGHTS-OF-WAY

In building a railway or a road through rolling terrain, economies of train or vehicle operation dictate that hills be cut through and that valleys be filled in. The cross-section area of the earth that must be moved to provide a right-of-way of width W for a road or railway has the general shape shown as BC (for "basic cut") or BF (for "basic fill") in Figure 12-1. To double the right-of-way requires moving additional earth with a cross-section area like MC (for "marginal cut") or MF (for "marginal fill") in this diagram.

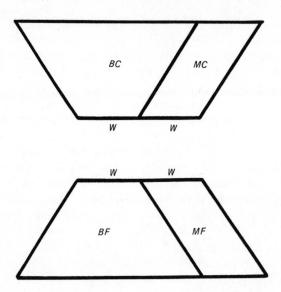

Figure 12-1. Effect of Increased Road Width on Earth Moving Costs

To suggest the orders of magnitude that are involved, suppose that soil conditions or design standards dictate that a cut have a slope equivalent to A feet horizontal for each foot of vertical rise (current Interstate System design standards call for A to be six, for example). Suppose also that a W foot right-of-way must make a level cut through a triangular shaped ridge and that the depth of this cut is H feet at the highest point on the ridge. Then it can be shown that the earth that must be moved for the basic cut is $2AH/3W$ times greater than the additional amount of earth that would have to be moved to double the width of the right-of-way.[f]

A two-lane rural road would generally be about 24 feet wide. Allowing for 8-foot shoulders and a few additional feet for drainage ditches on either

---

[f]If the bottom of the basic cut is W feet wide and its slope is A, its width at the top at a point where it is h feet deep is $W + 2Ah$. Its cross-section area at this point will therefore be $h[W + (W + 2Ah)]/2 = Wh + Ah^2$ while the cross-section area of the marginal cut will be simply Wh. With a triangular ridge, the height of the cut with a level base can be written $h = aD$ where D is the distance from the edge of the cut. Substituting aD for h in the formula for the cross-section area of the basic and marginal cuts, integrating between zero and $D*$ where $D*$ is the distance from the edge to the center of the cut, and substituting H and $Ad*$ yields $WD*H/2 + AD*H^2/3$ and $WD*H/2$ as the respective volumes of the basic and marginal cuts. Dividing the former expression by the latter gives the ratio, $1 + 2AH/3W$, reported in the text.

side of the road would result in a total right-of-way of perhaps 40 feet. Doubling this right-of-way would allow for a four-lane divided highway with a 16-foot median strip between the opposing traffic streams. If the cut is designed to Interstate standards (i.e., $A = 6$), $1 + 2AH/3W$ (total earth in the basic cut divided by total earth in the marginal cut) would equal two for a cut with a 10-foot maximum depth, three for a 20-foot cut, four for a 30-foot cut, and so forth. For $A = 3$, a design standard that is probably more common for rural roads, the corresponding ratios are 1.5, 2, 2.5, and so forth.

Doubling the width of a rural road would result not only in less than a doubling of total earth moving expenses, but would also considerably more than double the road's capacity. The U.S. Bureau of Public Roads' Highway Capacity Manual [8] (pp. 36-37) defines a highway's "basic capacity" as the maximum number of vehicles that can pass a given point during one hour under ideal conditions. The basic capacity of a straight, level, two-lane road with no signals or stop signs is 2,000 passenger cars per hour regardless of their distribution by direction. The basic capacity of a road with four or more lanes is 2,000 passenger cars per lane per hour. Thus, widening a rural road from two to four lanes results in a quadrupling of its capacity.

Geometric considerations also suggest there to be substantial scale economies in the provision of expressway capacity. A typical freeway contains paved shoulders on both sides of each set of traffic lanes, a median strip between opposing traffic streams, and buffer zones between the freeway and adjacent land. As a result, of the land area used by four- and eight-lane freeways with typical cross-sections, only about 33 and 50 percent respectively is devoted to freeway lanes themselves.

Determining the extent to which the scale economy implications of these geometric considerations are borne out in the real world is difficult. Four-lane expressways are generally built only in rural areas, small towns, and at the periphery of large urban centers. There, right-of-way costs are low and interchanges and overpasses tend to be far apart. Eight-lane expressways generally are built only near the central business districts of these areas. There, interchanges and overpasses are closely spaced. Also, right-of-way costs are high. As a result, minimizing the sum of right-of-way and construction costs dictates incurring increased construction costs to reduce right-of-way width by, for example, substituting concrete walls for sloped embankments, depressing the roadway and, on occasion, tunneling.

Because of the difficulties involved in separating the effects on construction costs of increased width taken by itself from those of the locations in which wider expressways are built, writers have expressed considerably different opinions on the extent and, indeed, even the existence of scale economies in freeway construction. For example, an analysis by Keeler et al. [3], (pp. 9-18) of 57 freeway segments in the San Francisco Bay Area supports the conclusion that freeway construction involves constant returns to road width.

Walters [7] (p. 184) notes that the average construction cost per mile for a sample of urban portions of the Interstate System collected by the Bureau of Public Roads and reported by Meyer, Kain, and Wohl [4] (henceforth MKW) on page 205 was $1.69 million for four-lane segments but $6 million for eight-lane segments. The MKW data also indicated an average cost per mile of $3.61 million for six-lane segments. Walters regards this evidence as suggesting "that there are increasing costs of construction in urban areas."

In what seems to me to be the most convincing analysis of the subject that has yet been published, MKW argue for the existence of quite substantial scale economies of width when the effect of expressway location is held fixed. Some rough data developed by them (pp. 200-211) can be interpreted as indicating that, around 1960, the annual cost at 6 percent of the capital invested in constructing one mile of an N lane urban freeway was approximately $Z = \$11,200 + \$2,500D + \$(7,200 + 300D)N$, where D, which appears to range between 10-300 in the United States, is the "net residential density" of the area through which the freeway passes, i.e., population per acre of land actually used for residential purposes. In addition, annual right-of-way costs were on the order of $0.005DZ$. Data privately supplied by the Federal Highway Administration (FHWA) indicate that maintenance costs averaged approximately $2,500 per lane mile of expressway in 1972. Between 1960 and the end of 1973 (the latest date for which an index value is available as this is written) the FHWA's composite highway construction cost index increased by a factor of 2.1. Its maintenance and operation cost index increased by a factor of 1.1 between 1972 and the end of 1973.

To repeat, the basic capacity of a four-lane expressway is about 2,000 vehicles per lane hour. Multiplying the MKW and FHWA annual cost data by the appropriate cost indices and dividing by 2,000 passenger cars per lane hour times 24 hours per day times 365 days per year yields the average and marginal costs per vehicle mile of expressway capacity shown in Table 12-1.

Table 12-1. Marginal and Average Costs of Highway Capacity in Areas of Different Net Residential Densities

Net Residential Density	Marginal Capacity Costs	Average Capacity Costs Number of Lanes		
		4	6	8
10	0.14¢	0.25¢	0.21¢	0.19¢
100	0.68¢	1.84¢	1.45¢	1.26¢
200	1.61¢	4.63¢	3.62¢	3.12¢
300	2.89¢	8.52¢	6.64¢	5.71¢

Source: See text.

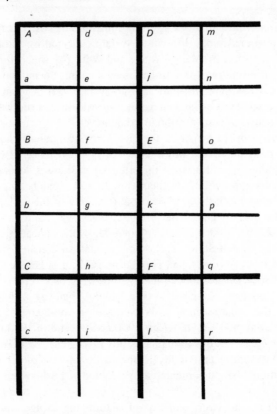

Figure 12-2. Effect of Expressway Density on Number of Required Interchanges

Thus far in the discussion of scale economies in the geometry of transportation rights-of-way, attention has been restricted to provision of single roads. A few words should also be said about the geometry of transportation networks. Here, it seems plausible to argue that *dis*economies of scale prevail. Figure 12-2 suggests why this is the case. Suppose that an expressway network is initially laid out on a two-mile rectangular grid (the thick lines in this figure). Each of the nine intersection of these roads—the points *A, B, C*, etc.—must necessarily involve an overpass and, more likely a full interchange.

Having completed this network, suppose that is is decided to double its capacity by converting it into a 1-mile rectangular grid. The new road represented by narrow lines result. Again, each intersection—the points *a, b, c*, etc.—must be provided with an overpass or an interchange. Note that addition of the dashed lines in Figure 12-2 substantially more than doubles the total number of intersections. Specifically, going from a 2- to a 1-mile grid increases this number from 9 to 36. Thus, a doubling of expressway capacity leads to a quadrupling of the number of intersections. More generally, the number of intersections in a rectangular grid of any given area is proportional to the square of the density of the lines it contains.[g]

The cost implications of the "square of the density" principle are quite significant. In 1960, the estimated average cost of an overpass and an interchange on the then uncompleted four-lane urban segments of the Interstate System in Minnesota was, respectively, $219,000 and $425,000. For comparison, the average estimated total cost per mile of these segments was $1.2 million (see Mohring [5], p. 249).[h]

THE "SQUARE ROOT PRINCIPLE" AND BUS LINE COSTS

In discussing the shape of railroad cost functions, Chapter Seven dealt in part with a problem that can be described in the following general terms: Customers desiring a service to be performed for them arrive at a place of business (a railroad yard or stops on a bus line, for example) at a steady rate of n per hour. Providing the service involves three sorts of costs: First is a fixed cost of F per batch (the costs of providing a bus and its driver or an engine, caboose, engineer, conductor, and front and rear brakemen, for example), which is independent of the number of customers served together. Second is a cost of S per customer, which is also independent of the number of customers in a batch. Third is a delay cost of V dollars per customer hour. This cost reflects the amount the average customer would be willing to pay to avoid a delay in being served and, for example, the cost to a railroad of providing the boxcars in which customers' goods are stored while awaiting service.

If service is provided to batches of N customers each, the interval between batches would be N/n hours. The average customer would wait half this inverval, $N/2n$ hours, and hence would incur a delay cost of $VN/2n$ dollars. Adding this cost to the direct cost of service, S, and an individual customers' share, F/N, of the fixed costs of a batch yields:

$$AC(n, N) = F/N + S + VN/2n \qquad (12\text{-}5)$$

as the average cost of serving a customer if n customers per hour demand service and if they are served in batches of N.

---

[g]I am indebted to William Vickrey for this point.

[h]In these calculations, an "urban" freeway segment is one that passes through any incorporated community. The $1.2 million per mile estimate therefore substantially understates the cost of "urban" highways as the term is commonly used.

Involved in this equation is the ability to trade customer delay costs for fixed costs per customer—an increase in N reduces F/N but increases $VN/2n$. N^*, the value of N that *minimizes* the sum of these costs, turns out to be:[i]

$$N^* = (2n\,F/V)^{\frac{1}{2}} \tag{12-6}$$

Thus, optimum batch size is proportional to the square root of the rate at which service is demanded. Using this expression to replace N in equation (12-5) yields:

$$AC^*(n) = (2V\,F/n)^{\frac{1}{2}} + S \tag{12-7}$$

as the minimum average cost of service if customers arrive at a rate of n per hour while

$$MC^*(n) = (VF/2n)^{\frac{1}{2}} + S \tag{12-8}$$

is the marginal cost of providing service at this rate.[j]

Note that the rate at which service is demanded enters into the denominator of one of the terms in each of these cost expressions. Therefore, average and marginal costs decline with increases in the rate at which the service is demanded; scale economies are involved. The relative magnitude of these scale economies is greatest when $S = 0$—i.e., when the only costs involved are the fixed costs of processing a batch on the one hand and delay costs on the other. Then, division of equation (12-8) by equation (12-6) reveals the marginal cost to be precisely half the average cost.[k]

A variety of common carrier transportation activities has attributes similar to those that lead to the square root principle of equation (12-6). As has already been suggested, examples include consolidation of boxcars arriving at the railroad yard Here into trains destined for There, and the provision of buses

[i]Found by differentiating $AC(n, N)$ with respect to N and setting the result to equal zero.

[j]Obtained by multiplying equation (12-7) by n to obtain total costs and then differentiating with respect to n.

[k]A few other features of the costs of providing a service of this type are worth mentioning at least parenthetically. Substituting equation (12-6) into equation (12-5) reveals that cost minimization dictates the equality of fixed costs per customer and delay costs per customer. Multiplying equations (12-5) and (12-8) by N^* yields, respectively, total costs per batch and the total revenues that would be collected if marginal cost prices were charged for the services. Comparison of the resulting expressions reveals that revenues under these circumstances would exactly cover variable customer costs, SN^*, plus delay costs. However, they would yield no contribution to F, the fixed costs of a batch.

to travelers waiting for service along a bus route. Airline service between two cities provides another example. Travelers differ in their desired departure and arrival times. By scheduling large planes infrequently, an airline can take advantage of the scale economies suggested by equations (12-1) through (12-4). It can do so, however, only at the expense of greater delays to its customers and the risk of losing some of them to other airlines which provide more frequent service.

Data permitting the quantification of railroad scale economies are not readily available. The optimization of airline schedules will be discussed later in this chapter as an example of massed reserve scale economies. Attention here will be restricted to the scale economies involved in providing bus service.[1] Before proceeding to a discussion of the nature and magnitude of these scale economies, the implications of scale economies for the relationship between transportation prices and costs warrant explanation.

Consider first the relationship between costs and the revenues that would be generated by marginal cost prices if the production of widgets involves increasing returns to scale. Suppose that producing them requires two inputs, labor and capital, and that the long run marginal and average cost schedules associated with this process are as drawn in Figure 12-3. Suppose also that the widget demand schedule (not drawn, to avoid clutter) intersects the long run marginal cost schedule at C.

To minimize the cost of producing OQ widgets per week would require employing that amount of capital that would generate the short run marginal and average variable cost schedules shown passing through points C and B respectively. Setting price equal to long run (equals short run) marginal cost would then yield revenues of $OFCQ$ per week. These revenues would suffice to cover the total costs of labor inputs, $OACQ$ (= $OEBQ$). In addition, they would yield quasi-rents of ACF (= $EBCF$) on capital inputs. These quasi-rents would fall short of the weekly costs of capital inputs. Specifically, since this cost is $EBDG$ (= ACH), a subsidy of $FCDG$ (= FCH) would be required to cover total costs.

It would make no difference whether the widget manufacturer used his subsidy check to pay interest on his debts or to cover part of his wage bill. Still, for the purpose at hand, it is important to recognize that the required subsidy equals precisely the amount by which the costs of the fixed inputs he supplies exceed the quasi-rents generated in the process of simultaneously minimizing production costs and setting price equal to short run marginal cost.

Figure 12-3 can be used without alteration to describe bus operations that are subject to increasing returns. The only difference in interpretation stems from the fact that, with buses, inputs are provided by travelers, not just by the bus company that serves them. Suppose that H is the number of bus

---

[1]A more extended discussion of the subject is contained in Mohring [6].

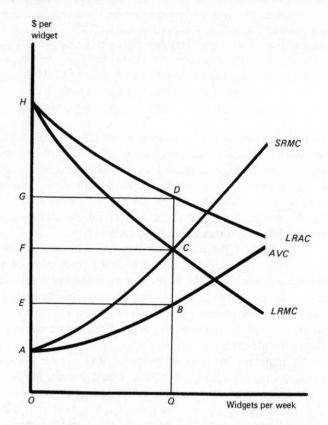

Figure 12-3. Short and Long Run Cost Relationships with Economies of Scale

hours of service required to provide that number of bus trips that minimizes the sum of the dollar costs incurred by bus companies and the time costs incurred by travelers when *OQ* trips per week are taken. Given this level of service, the time cost borne directly by a traveler is *QB*.

When a representative traveler boards and alights, he slows the bus on which he travels by the amount of time the doors must be left open to serve him and by the time required to make an additional stop if no one else desires service at his origin or destination. Since a representative customer provides time inputs values at *QB*, setting the price he pays equal to the short run marginal cost of his trip would require levying on him a fare—a "congestion toll"—equal to *BC*. If such short run marginal cost fares were charged, *EBCF* would be a quasi-rent to bus services, just as in the widget case. In both cases the required subsidy, *FCDG*, is the amount by which this rent falls short of the costs of fixed inputs.

Turning to the nature of the scale economies involved in providing bus service, consider a segment of a "steady state" bus route. Along each mile of the route:

An average of B people per hour board and B exit from buses. Their origins and destinations are uniformly distributed along the route[m]

M is the length of each person's trip. Hence, at any point along the route segment, an average of MB/X travelers are aboard each bus where

X (to be optimized) is the number of buses that traverse the route segment each hour[n]

C dollars per hour is the cost of providing the services of a bus

Y (also to be optimized) is the number of uniformly spaced bus stops per mile

g is the speed at which travelers walk to and from bus stops

b times the headway between buses is the average length of a passenger's wait for service once he reaches a stop

V dollars is the average value passengers place on an hour spent aboard a bus while

aV is the average value they attach to time spent walking to and from bus stops and waiting for buses to come. Empirical work discussed in Chapter Five suggests a to be substantially greater than 1

---

[m]More precisely, origins and destinations are assumed to be uniformly distributed either along the route on which the bus travels or on a continuum of parallel streets which intersect that route.

[n]Actually, the bus company cannot control X but rather only the number of bus hours of service provided to the route. Because the number of passengers demanding service is a random variable, the number of bus trips that can be provided with any given number of bus hours is also random. In this analysis, the stochastic nature of the system is, to a considerable degree, ignored. Taking stochastic elements fully into account would have made both analysis and exposition considerably more complex but—hopefully—would not have affected the results appreciably.

S miles per hour is the overall average speed of a bus while

$S*$ is the speed at which it travels when not engaged in stopping and starting maneuvers

f hours are required to board or unload a passenger once the bus has stopped and its doors have been opened

d hours are added to the time required for a bus to traverse the route segment by each stopping and starting maneuver

The total hourly costs of providing service to an M mile segment of this route can be broken into four components: bus company operating costs and the costs to passengers of walking time, waiting time, and time in transit. It takes M/S hours for the average bus to traverse the route segment. Since X buses per hour do so, at a cost of C dollars per bus hour, total bus company costs are CXM/S per hour, and the cost per expected passenger served is CX/BS. The distance between stops is $1/Y$ miles. The maximum walk for any passenger is half this distance.

If origins and destinations are uniformly distributed between stops, the average passenger would walk $1/4Y$ miles both to and from a stop, or a total of $1/2Y$ miles. The cost of such a walk is $aV/2gY$ dollars. The average cost per passenger of time spent waiting at a stop is aVb/X dollars, while that of time in transit is MV/S dollars. Summing these four cost components gives the total cost per expected passenger for the steady state route:

$$Z = CX/BS + aV/2gV + MV/S + aVb/X \qquad (12\text{-}9)$$

If overall bus speed, S, were independent of X, the rate at which bus service is provided, equation (12-9) would have exactly the same form as equation (12-5), which leads to the square root principle. The first term on the right of each of these equations is the fixed cost of providing the service divided by the number of customers. The last term is the delay costs per customer, which in each case depends only on the frequency of service. Finally, the middle term(s) are those costs that are proportional to the number of passengers served. Not surprisingly, then, *if* bus speed were independent of the rate at which bus service is provided, the number of buses per hour that would minimize equation (12-9) is proportional to the square root of the demand for bus service. Specifically,

$$X* = [aVbSB/C]^{\frac{1}{2}} \qquad (12\text{-}10)$$

But the speed at which a bus travels does depend on the number of passengers it carries. Holding fixed the rate at which travelers demand service, an increase in the number of buses per hour would reduce the number of passengers carried by each bus. It would therefore reduce both the frequency and the duration of the stops made to board and discharge passengers. This being the case, determining the service characteristics that will minimize costs requires specifying the relationship between realized speed, S, on the one hand and X, Y, S^*, and the remaining parameters of the system on the other. In each route mile, a total of B travelers per hour board and B leave X buses at Y or fewer stops. Hence, the average number of passengers that board or leave any one bus at any one stop is $m = 2B/XY$.

It seems reasonable to suppose that the actual number of passengers desiring service at a bus stop satisfies the conditions discussed in Chapter Seven under which the Poisson distribution applies. If so, then the probability that r people will board or alight from a given bus at any one stop is $P[r] = e^{-m} m^r/r!$ The probability that a given stop will be made is $1 - P[0]$, the probability that no one will either wish to alight or be at that stop when the bus arrives, i.e., $1 - e^{-m}$. The expected number of stops per mile is Y times this fraction. The expected time to travel 1 mile, $1/X$, can therefore be written as the sum of the time actually absorbed in travel. $1/S^*$, the time required to board and unload $2B/X$ passengers and the time absorbed by the expected number of starting and stopping maneuvers:

$$1/S = 1/S^* + 2Bf/X + dY\,[1 - e^{-m}] \tag{12-11}$$

Quite messy algebra is involved in determining the number of buses per hour that would minimize costs as given by equations (12-9) and (12-11) and the average and marginal costs of trips that would result from providing that level of service. Little point would be served by reproducing this algebra here.[o] Let it suffice to say that, given an assumption about the number of allowable stops and values of the various parameters these equations contain, computer programs can be written to determine optimum service levels and the resulting costs. The specific parameter values employed reflect cost conditons in the Twin Cities Metropolitan Area during the early 1970s. They are:[p]

M = (average) trip length: 3 miles

[o]Because costs are quite insensitive to changes in Y for many combinations of Y and B values, it is impossible to solve simultaneously for the cost minimizing values of X and Y. The procedure used in deriving the numerical values described below involves employing Newton's method to find the value of X that sets equal to zero the derivative with respect to X of the system defined by equations (12-9) and (12-11) for each of a variety of stop spacings and trip demand levels.

[p]The appendix to Mohring [6] describes the reasons for choosing these values.

g = walking speed: 3 miles per hour

b = wait for service as fraction of bus headway: 0.5

V = value of time in transit: $1.00 per hour

aV = value of walking and waiting time: $3.00 per hour

$S*$ = bus speed when not stopping or starting: 20 miles per hour

f = time to board or unload passenger: 1.8 seconds

d = time to stop and start bus at bus stop: 18 seconds

C = cost of a bus hour's services: $12.75 during morning and afternoon peak; $5.60 at other times.

During most of the day, about the same number of people travel in each direction on real-world urban bus routes. During morning peak hours, however, substantially more people travel toward than away from the central business district. During afternoon peak hours, the reverse is true. Numerical calculations were therefore carried out both for balanced flows and for routes on which five times as many people travel in one direction as in the other. Some of the results of these calculations are spelled out in Tables 12-2 and 12-3.

To repeat, equation (12-8) indicates that the optimum service frequency would be proportional to the square root of the demand for service *if* the rate at which travelers board a bus has no effect on the speed at which it operates. That is, denoting alternative values of passengers per mile-hour by B_1 and B_2 and the associated optimum service frequencies by X_1 and X_2, equation (12-8) indicates that $E = 0.5$ in the expression[q]

$$X_1/X_2 = (B_1/B_2)^E$$

Unfortunately, no such simple rule can be derived from Table 12-2. The E values that result from comparing optimum service levels for nine and 150 passengers per mile per hour range between 0.51 when peak period cost conditions and eight stops per mile are assumed and 0.70 under the assumption of off-peak service levels and sixteen stops per mile. Still, although no simple rule can be given, Table 12-2 does rather strongly suggest that an increase in the demand for bus service should be accompanied by a less than proportionate increase in

[q]In this expression, E can be interpreted as the arc of elasticity of the optimum service level with respect to the travel rate.

Table 12-2. Optimum Service Levels, Fares, and Subsidies for Three-Mile Trips on Steady State Bus Routes

| | Off-Peak Conditions | | | Peak Period Conditions | | | | | | |
| | | | | Uniform Flow | | | Uneven Flow | | | |
Average Passengers per Mile Hour	Buses per Hour	Fare	Subsidy per Passenger	Buses per Hour	Fare	Subsidy per Passenger	Buses per Hour	Main Fare	Back Fare	Subsidy per Passenger
Eight Stops Allowed per Mile										
150	41	8.3¢	3.6¢	21	9.2¢	7.1¢	21	7.3¢	13.0¢	7.1¢
90	29	8.4	5.2	16	10.3	9.3	16	8.0	13.3	9.4
45	19	8.3	8.1	11	11.5	13.5	11	9.4	13.7	13.7
21	12	8.1	12.7	7	12.6	20.3	7	10.9	13.9	20.3
9	7	7.8	20.4	5	13.3	31.7	5	12.3	13.9	31.6
Sixteen Stops Allowed per Mile										
150	50	11.5¢	3.0¢	29	17.6¢	5.2¢	29	17.0¢	16.2¢	5.2¢
90	33	11.2	4.5	20	17.6	7.5	20	17.4	16.0	7.4
45	20	10.5	7.4	13	17.4	12.0	13	17.6	15.7	11.7
21	12	9.7	12.2	8	16.9	19.1	8	17.6	15.3	18.7
9	7	8.9	20.1	5	16.4	30.8	5	17.1	15.0	30.4

Table 12-3.   Costs for Three-Mile Trips on Optimized Steady State Bus Routes

| Average Passengers per Mile Hour | Off Peak Conditions | | Peak Period Conditions | | | | |
| | | | Uniform Flow | | Uneven Flow | | |
	Average Cost	Marginal Cost	Average Cost	Marginal Cost	Average Cost	Main Marginal Cost	Back Marginal Cost
Eight Stops Allowed per Mile							
150	45¢	41¢	57¢	50¢	57¢	50¢	47¢
90	47	42	61	51	61	52	49
45	52	44	69	55	69	56	52
21	60	47	81	61	82	62	58
9	73	53	103	71	104	72	69
Sixteen Stops Allowed per Mile							
150	44¢	41¢	59¢	54¢	62¢	59¢	45¢
90	46	42	62	55	65	60	46
45	50	43	69	57	71	62	49
21	57	45	81	62	83	66	55
9	71	51	102	71	103	74	65

bus frequencies. This finding is in sharp contrast with what seems to be common operating practice of most urban bus operations—to allocate buses among routes so as to make service frequency proportional to demand.

Tables 12-2 and 12-3 suggest quite substantial scale economies to exist in the provision of bus service. The ratios of the marginal trip costs listed in Table 12-3 to the corresponding average costs range between about 70 percent for nine passengers per mile per hour (about the demand level during off-peak periods in the Twin Cities Metropolitan Area) and about 90 percent for 150 passengers per mile per hour (a level considerably higher than that experienced on almost any urban bus route in the United States). Depending on the specific cost parameters and stop spacings assumed, an increase from 9 to 150 passengers per mile per hour would result in a 38-45 percent reduction in the average cost of a bus trip.

The size of the subsidy required if costs are to be minimized and marginal cost fares charged varies with cost conditions, stop spacings, and (most important) level of demand. Regardless of the assumptions made about these parameters, however, the required subsidies are substantial. The lowest ratio of subsidy per passenger to bus company operating costs per passenger (determined by adding the subsidy per passenger to the marginal cost fare) revealed by Table 12-2 is 21 percent for 150 passengers per mile per hour and 16 stops per mile under off-peak cost conditions. For nine passengers per mile per hour and 8 stops per mile, the subsidy-operating cost ratios range between 70 and 72 percent.

Although not directly related to the basic purpose of this chapter—describing and quantifying transportation scale economies—it is worth touching briefly on some surprising features of the results summarized by Tables 12-2 and 12-3 for the uneven flow conditions that characterize peak hour operations in most urban areas and on some other results that are not reflected in these tables. First, when five times as many people travel in one direction as in the other, the average cost per passenger carried is only slightly greater than would be the case if the same total number of passengers was distributed evenly between directions. Under peak period cost conditions, average costs per passenger for uneven flows in Table 12-3 range between 1-5 percent more than those for uniform flows. Similarly, the differences between the long run marginal costs of main- and back-haul trips are also surprisingly small.

The reason for these small cost differentials is related to the paradoxical results shown in the ninth and tenth columns of Table 12-2. For 8 (or fewer) allowable stops per mile, the marginal cost fare for a trip is greater in the back-haul than in the main-haul direction. The explanation for these curious results seems to be as follows. By slowing down the bus he boards, an additional back-haul traveler directly affects only one-fifth as many other travelers as does an additional main-haul traveler. But since so few passengers per mile board the average back-haul bus, the probability that adding a passenger will require an additional stop to be made is much greater for the back than for the main haul.

Under the assumed conditions, it takes 11 times as long (19.8 as opposed to 1.8 seconds) to board a passenger if a special stop must be made for him than it would take if the stop would have been made in the absence of his trip. By reducing operating speed and hence the number of trips that can be made with any given number of bus hours per hour, additional stops affect all travelers, not just those aboard the bus in question. When appreciably fewer than one stop is made per passenger boarded, it would appear that this system effect of an additional back-haul traveler more than offsets the smaller number of people directly affected by his trip.

Going through the arithmetic of a specific example may be worthwhile in this connection. During morning and afternoon peaks, approximately 50 and 10 passengers per mile per hour, respectively, board main- and back-haul buses on the average Twin Cities route. To cite results that are not incorporated in Tables 12-2 and 12-3, if stops are spaced one-eigth of a mile apart, the cost minimizing service frequency for this output level is 8.88 buses per hour. With this service level, 16.9 and 3.4 passengers, respectively, would be aboard the average main- and back-haul bus.

The "own bus effect" of an additional main-haul trip (i.e., the cost it imposes on passengers already on the bus boarded by the additional traveler) accounts for 5.8 of the 10.2-cent marginal cost fare; the "system effect" (i.e., the cost the marginal traveler imposes on travelers other than those aboard the bus that carries him by reducing the number of trips that can be provided with any given number of bus hours of service) for the remaining 4.4 cents. The corresponding back-haul figures are: fare, 13.8 cent; own bus effect, 2.9 cents; and system effect, 10.9 cents. The substantial difference between the two system effects reflects the fact that the probability that boarding an additional passenger will require an additional stop, e^{-m}, is 0.755 for the back haul but only 0.245 for the main haul.

A point implicit in the foregoing should be made explicit. Stop spacing is a far more important determinant of optimum fares than is the rate at which trips are taken. Thus (again to cite data that are not tabulated), under peak load cost-even travel rate conditions, marginal cost fares for the steady state route only vary between 2.2 and 3.5 cents over the range 9-150 passengers per mile per hour when one stop per mile is allowed. At the other extreme, marginal cost fares vary between 19.9 and 26.7 cents over this range of outputs when a separate stop is made for each passenger.

Although not as dramatic as with fares, stop spacing has a substantial effect on optimum bus headways and hence on the bus operating and travel time components of total costs. These effects are particularly great for high trip output rates. Thus, under peak load cost-even flow conditions, the optimum service level for the steady state route with 150 passengers per mile-hour is 20.4 buses per hour when one stop per mile is allowed, 28.7 for 16 stops per mile, and 39.0 when a separate stop is made for each passenger. Bus company operating costs are 10.8, 22.9, and 30.6 cents per passenger under these alternative service rates, and the respective travel time costs for a three-mile trip are 76, 36, and 35 cents.

With few passengers per mile-hour—i.e., for small values of B—the sum of travel time and bus operating costs is a minimum if buses stop for each passenger thereby eliminating time spent walking to a bus stop. For large B values, between 4-8 stops per mile are optimum. Finally, for a narrow range of intermediate values, 16, 32, or 64 allowable stops would minimize total costs. Where the dividing lines between "small," "intermediate," and "large" values of B are drawn depends, of course, on the specific values given system parameters.

As the travel time value used decreases, the dividing lines occur at smaller and smaller B values. On the other hand, decreases in trips lengths and in bus operating costs serve to increase these dividing lines. Thus, for off-peak cost conditions, stopping on demand proved optimal for the steady state route even for the largest value of B tested, 250 passengers per mile-hour. However, for peak period cost conditions, 4-8 stops per mile provide minimum costs with 45 or more passengers per mile-hour. With B equal to 30—the present peak hour average in the Twin Cities—16 stops per mile is optimum, although average total costs for 8, 16, 32, and 64 stops as well as stopping for each traveler all lie between 74.7 cents and 75.0 cents.

MASSED RESERVES SCALE
ECONOMIES AND AIRLINE SCHEDULING

Chapter Seven introduced the concepts of *expected* demand and *expected* cost in dealing with situations in which the demand for a commodity involves elements of randomness. The expected demand for a commodity at a given price is simply the average rate (say D^*) at which it would be sold if that price is charged. If production during a time period must equal the quantity actually demanded during that period, the expected cost (call it C^*) of producing at an expected level of D^* can be found by (1) multiplying the actual cost of producing each possible quantity by the probability of that quantity's being demanded and (2) summing the results of these multiplications over all possible demand levels.

The Eastern Airlines shuttle service between Boston and New York was used to illustrate these concepts. Eastern requires no reservations for this service: it quarantees a seat at the scheduled time for all who appear at the departure gate. If the travelers who demand seats on a particular flight exceed the capacity of the assigned aircraft, a second, standby aircraft is called into service.

In this illustration, it was assumed that, on average, four people demand seats on the 9:00 a.m. Wednesday flight[r] from Boston to New York.

---

[r]In the discussion of this section, the term "9:00 a.m. Wednesday flights" is used as shorthand for "a group of flights that are subject to identical underlying demand conditions". On virtually every U.S. airline, the average demand for service on the Wednes-

Also assume, to modify the Chapter Seven example slightly, that service must be provided in four-passenger aircraft at a cost, F dollars per flight, which is independent of the number of passengers carried. Finally, suppose again that, as is normal for random processes of this sort, the demand for seats on the shuttle is characterized by the Poisson distribution. If so, the probabilities that zero, 1-4, 5-8, and 9-12 passengers will demand service on any given Wednesday are respectively 1.8, 61.1, 35.0, and 2.1 percent. The probability that more than twelve passengers will arrive on any given Wednesday is so small that this possibility can be ignored. With these probabilities and a cost per aircraft flight of F dollars, the expected cost of the 9:00 a.m. Wednesday flight is

$$0.018 \times 0 + 0.611 \times F + 0.350 \times 2F + 0.021 \times 3F = 1.373\ F$$

Now suppose that the expected demand for service on the 9:00 a.m. Wednesday shuttle suddenly doubles but that Eastern must continue to serve these travelers with four-passenger aircraft.[s] If the expected demand for the flight is eight passengers, the probability that no one will demand service on any given Wednesday is less than .05 percent. The probabilities that 1-4, 5-8, 9-12, 13-16, and 17-20 travelers will demand service are, respectively, 9.9, 49.3, 34.4, 6.0, and 0.4 percent. Multiplying these probabilities by the corresponding numbers of required planes yields an expected cost of $2.374\ F$. Thus, a doubling of expected demand leads only to a 72.9 percent increase in expected costs: $2.374\ F/1.273\ F = 1.729$.

This economy of scale is closely related to Florence's "principle of multiples" that was described in the introduction to this chapter. It is, after all, only the last aircraft that Eastern calls into service which has a chance of departing with empty seats. The larger is the number of full aircraft which preceded this last aircraft, the larger is the number of passengers over which its unutilized capacity is averaged.

Eastern's Boston-New York-Washington shuttle is unusual among the services offered by scheduled airlines. It is a far more common practice to provide at a specified time a single aircraft on which advanced reservations may be made. If the number seeking reservations on such a flight exceeds the capacity of the aircraft, the excess passengers are not provided with a standby aircraft. Rather, they must seek seats aboard other flights that depart earlier or later than does their first choice.

---

day immediately preceding Thanksgiving is greater than that on, say, the third Wednesday in July. In turn, on most airlines, average demand is greater on the third Wednesday in July than on the second Wednesday in February. These systematic seasonal variations in demand levels are ignored in what follows.

[s]This assumption rules out the possibility of taking advantage of the scale economies in aircraft size discussed in the first section.

Two sorts of potential delays are associated with this common scheduling practice. First is the "frequency delay." It results from the fact that a traveler's desired departure time rarely coincides exactly with that of the airline schedule. Second is the "stochastic delay."[t] It results if the traveler's most preferred flight is booked to capacity and he must therefore take a flight that is, for him, less desirable.

Holding fixed the number of passengers per day desiring service between two points, frequency delays can be reduced by providing more frequent departures. Stochastic delays can be lowered by using larger aircraft, thereby increasing the ratio of seats available to expected passengers. Both procedures for reducing traveler delays are costly, of course. If it is correct to infer from equations (12-1) through (12-4) that the cost of an aircraft block hour increases with the 0.75 power of its seating capacity, providing 300 seats per day in two 150-seat aircraft would cost 19 percent more than providing this capacity in a single 300-seat aircraft ($2 \times 150^{0.75}/300^{0.75} = 1.19$). Similarly, providing a 200-seat aircraft would cost 24 percent more than providing one with 150 seats ($200^{0.75}/150^{0.75} = 1.24$).

The optimum combination of average load factor (i.e., the average ratio of passengers to seats provided) and flight frequency would be that which would minimize the sum of airline operating costs and the costs to travelers of the delays involved in being required to depart at other than their most preferred times. A variety of factors enter into the computation of this optimum combination for any given origin-destination pair. These factors include the cost penalties associated with more frequent departures and lower load factors, the daily average number of passengers, their distribution of desired departure times, the amount the average passenger would be willing to pay to avoid an hour's delay,[u] and the length of the flight. Regarding this last mentioned factor, the total cost of providing an additional empty seat and the total cost penalty associated with flying small rather than large aircraft is greater on long than on short flights. For this reason, the optimum average delay would increase with length of flight.

Without going into detail about the quite complex calculations needed to take these factors into account in optimizing aircraft schedules and sizes, it can be seen that this optimization process involves economies of scale. Suppose that the airline schedules between Here and There have taken these factors into account in an optimum fashion and that the average daily demand for service between these two cities suddenly doubles. The optimum response to

---

[t]The terms "frequency delay" and "stochastic delay" are borrowed from Douglas and Miller [2], some of whose results are summarized below.

[u]The value of delay time to a traveler is probably *not* the same as the value to him of travel time. Rather, it seems reasonable to argue that the latter value is an upper bound to the former. This relationship between the two values seems likely if only because a traveler can undertake a greater range of activities during the interval between his desired and actual departure times than during the period in which he actually travels.

this increase in demand would be a combination of increased frequency of scheduled departures and increased average size of aircraft used. The result would be both smaller average passenger delays and lower operating costs per passenger.

To illustrate the massed reserves aspect of the scale economies involved in providing Here-There air service, it is useful to suppose that the airlines do not respond in this optimum fashion. Rather, suppose that they increase the size of aircraft and the frequency of flights only by enough to leave the average delay per passenger unchanged. Accomplishing this objective in response to a doubling of demand would require less than a doubling of the aircraft capacity assigned to Here-There service.

This is true for two reasons. First, suppose that additional seats are at least partially provided by scheduling additional aircraft. Then a traveler who finds that his most desired departure is booked to capacity will be faced by a shorter wait for the next Here-There departure than was the case prior to the increase in demand. If the increase in demand is accompanied by a less than proportionate increase in seats provided, load factors naturally increase. A higher average load factor means a greater probability that a stochastic delay will occur, i.e., a greater chance that any given flight will be booked to capacity. However, schedules can be adjusted so that the resulting increase in the probability that a passenger will experience a stochastic delay is offset by a reduction in the average length of that delay which leaves average delay time per passenger unchanged.

Second (and here is where the principle of massed reserves comes in), suppose that it is desired to hold fixed the probability that a traveler desiring a seat on, say, the 9:00 a.m. Wednesday Here-There flight will not find one available. Doing so in response to a doubling of the average level of demand for the flight would require less than a doubling of the capacity of the aircraft assigned to it. Showing why this is the case requires further discussion of the properties of the Poisson distribution. This is the distribution which, to repeat, seems most nearly applicable to describing such phenomena as variations among Wednesdays in the demand for 9:00 a.m. flights and among weekdays in those who arrive at a particular bus stop between 9:00 and 9:05 a.m.

The variance[v] and the average of a Poisson distribution are equal. If a large number of 9:00 a.m. Wednesday flights is observed, the number of passengers demanding services will be found to lie within one standard deviation (defined as the square root of the variance) of the average number of passengers

---

[v]For a discrete distribution like the Poisson, if $P(X)$ is the probability that, for example, X passengers will demand service on any given 9:00 a.m. Wednesday flight and m is the average number of 9:00 a.m. Wednesday passengers, the variance of the distribution of passengers for this flight is the sum of $P(X) \cdot (X - m)^2$ over all possible values of X.

approximately 68 percent of the time.[w] Thus, if average demand is 81 passengers, the number actually requesting service on a series of Wednesdays would lie within the range $\pm 81^{\frac{1}{2}}/81 = \pm 11$ percent of the average approximately 68 percent of the time. If average demand doubles to 162 passengers, the corresponding range is $\pm 162^{\frac{1}{2}}/162 = \pm 7.9$ percent.

Suppose, to carry the calculations one step further, that it is desired to provide seats sufficient to assure that only 1 percent of all 9:00 a.m. Wednesday flights will be booked to capacity and hence that passengers desiring service must be turned away from only 1 percent of these flights. For an average demand of 81 passengers, approximately a 102-seat aircraft would be required to achieve this objective. For an average demand of 162 passengers, approximately 192 seats would be required—only 88 percent more than for an average demand of 81 passengers.[x]

Douglas and Miller [2], (ch. 6) have analyzed the scheduling practices that would minimize the sum of airline operating costs and the costs to passengers of frequency and stochastic delays. The model they develop is too complex to warrant attempting to summarize its characteristics here. Suffice it to say that their analysis takes into account most of the scheduling scale economies discussed in this section. It does not, however, fully incorporate the possibility of relating the size of aircraft employed to a market's level of demand or distance.[y] Therefore, the magnitude of aggregate scheduling scale economies is probably understated by the entries in Table 12-4, which summarize their results under the assumption that the average traveler would be willing to pay $10 to avoid an hour of frequency or stochastic delays.[z]

[w]Strictly speaking, this statement and the calculations which follow apply only to those passengers who have the 9:00 a.m. Wednesday flight as their first choice. On some days, those demanding seats on this flight also include travelers whose first choice flight was booked to capacity. The calculations required to take this second group of passengers into account are considerably more complex that those described here (see Douglas and Miller [2], ch. 6), but would not lead to significantly different results.

"Approximately 68 percent of the time" is derived from the fact that if the average of a Poisson distribution is fairly large, its values are closely approximated by those of a normal distribution. For such a distribution, in turn, approximately 68 percent of the observations drawn in a large sample will fall within one standard deviation of the mean.

[x]Continuing to rely on the normal approximation to a Poisson distribution, the probability is 0.99 that an observation drawn from this distribution will lie between zero and a value equal to the mean plus 2.33 standard deviations. $81 + (81)^{\frac{1}{2}} \times 2.33 = 102$ and $162 + (162)^{\frac{1}{2}} \times 2.33 = 192$.

[y]Douglas and Miller [2] assume that a Douglas DC8 is used for all flights of 1,600 or more miles, a DC9 for 100-passenger markets of between 100-1,000 miles, and a Boeing 727 for all other markets.

[z]Douglas and Miller [2] also worked with the alternative assumption that delay time is valued at $5 an hour. Their results under this assumption are quite similar to those shown in Table 12-4. Optimum load factors for this delay time value are 2-4 percent

According to this table, minimizing the sum of airline and traveler delay costs would result in airline costs per coach passenger of $22.64 and $16.62 for 200-mile markets with averages of 100 and 6,400 passengers per day respectively. Thus a 64-fold increase in demand would result in a 20 percent reduction in costs per passenger. These scale economies are somewhat smaller for longer markets. At distances of 2,600 miles, for example, a 64-fold increase in demand is associated with only a 15 percent reduction in average costs.

---

greater than those shown while optimum airline costs are 4–6 percent and 1–2 percent less for 100- and 6,400-passenger-per-day markets, respectively.

Table 12-4.   Variations in Optimum Average Load Factors and Airline Costs per Coach Passenger with Market Sizes and Distances (Delay Time Value = $10 per hour)

| | Length of Trip (Miles) | | | | | | | |
| | 200 | | 1000 | | 1800 | | 2600 | |
Average Daily Passengers	Load Factor	Cost per Passenger	Load Factor	Cost per Passenger	Load Factor	Cost per Passenger	Load Factor	Cost per Passenger
100	44%	$22.64	50%	$55.20	57%	$81.06	59%	$107.70
400	54	19.16	60	47.02	64	75.20	66	100.28
1600	61	17.75	66	44.31	71	70.49	72	95.07
6400	68	16.62	72	42.04	76	67.65	77	91.34

Source: Douglas and Miller [2], Chapter 6.

References

CHAPTER ONE

1. H.C. Bos and L.M. Koyck. "The Appraisal of Road Construction Projects: A Practical Example." *The Review of Economics and Statistics* 43 (February 1961): 13–20.
2. Robert T. Brown and Clell G. Harral. "Estimating Highway Benefits in Underdeveloped Countries." *Highway Research Record* 115 (1965): 29–43.
3. Paul J. Garfield and Wallace F. Lovejoy. *Public Utility Economics* (Englewood Cliffs, N.J.: Prentice-Hall, 1964).
4. Benjamin Higgins. *Economic Development* (New York: W.W. Norton, 1959).
5. John R. Meyer et al. *The Economics of Competition in the Transportation Industries* (Cambridge, Mass.: Harvard University Press, 1959).
6. William Miller, *Metropolitan Rapid Transit Financing.* A Report to the Metropolitan Rapid Transit Survey of New York and New Jersey (Princeton, N.J., 1957).
7. J. Tinbergen. "The Appraisal of Road Construction: Two Calculation Schemes." *The Review of Economics and Statistics* 39 (August 1957): 241–249.
8. U.S. Bureau of Public Roads. *Final Report of the Highway Cost Allocation Study* (Washington, D.C.: U.S. Government Printing Office, 1961), Part IV.

CHAPTER TWO

1. William Baumol. *Economic Theory and Operations Analysis.* 2d ed. (Englewood Cliffs, N.J.: Prentice-Hall, 1965).
2. C.E. Ferguson and J.P. Gould. *Microeconomic Theory.* 4th ed. (Homewood, Ill.: Richard D. Irwin, 1975).

3. Edwin Mansfield. *Microeconomics: Theory and Applications.* 2d ed. (New York: W.W. Norton, 1975).

CHAPTER THREE

1. R.R. Coleman. "A Study of Urban Travel Times in Pennsylvania Cities." *Highway Research Board Bulletin* 306 (1961): 39–63.
2. Herbert Mohring. "Relationship Between Optimum Congestion Tolls and Present Highway User Charges." *Highway Research Record* 47 (1964): 1–14.
3. American Association of State Highway Officials, Committee on Highway Planning and Design Policies. *Road User Benefits for Highway Improvements* (Washington, D.C., 1960), pp. 100–126.

CHAPTER FOUR

1. William Miller. *Metropolitan Rapid Transit Financing.* A Report to the Metropolitan Rapid Transit Survey of New York and New Jersey (Princeton, N.J., 1957).
2. Herbert Mohring. "Urban Highway Investments." In Robert Dorfman, ed. *Measuring Benefits of Government Investments* (Washington, D.C.: Brookings Institution, 1965), pp. 231–291.
3. Robert Strotz. "Urban Transportation Parables." In Julius Margolis, ed. *The Public Economy of Urban Communities* (Washington, D.C.: Resources for the Future, 1965), pp. 127–169.
4. American Association of State Highway Officials, Committee on Highway Planning and Design Policies. *Road User Benefits for Highway Improvements* (Washington, D.C., 1960), pp. 100–126.

CHAPTER FIVE

1. M.E. Beesley. "The Value of Time Spent in Travelling: Some New Evidence." *Economica* (May 1965): 174–185.
2. B.M. Cope and C.L. Gauthier. *Cost of Operating an Automobile* (Washington, D.C.: U.S. Bureau of Public Roads), February 1970.
3. Reuben Gronau. *The Value of Time in Passenger Transportation: The Demand for Air Travel.* Occasional Paper 109 (New York: National Bureau for Economic Research, 1970).
4. Thomas E. Lisco. *The Value of Commuters' Travel Time: A Study in Urban Transportation.* Ph.D. Dissertation, University of Chicago, 1967.
5. Allan Maslove. *The Value of Commuters' Travel Time in a Multi-Nodal City.* Ph.D. Dissertation, University of Minnesota, 1972.

6. Herbert Mohring. "Land Values and the Measurement of Highway Benefits." *Journal of Political Economy* 69 (June 1961): 236–249.

7. _____. "Spatial Equilibrium in a CBD Oriented City." In Ronald Grieson, ed. *Essays in Urban Economics and Public Finance in Honor of William S. Vickrey* (Lexington, Mass.: Heath-Lexington Books, 1976).

8. William C. Pendleton. *The Value of Highway Accessibility.* Ph.D. Dissertation, University of Chicago, 1963.

9. Robley Winfrey. *Economic Analysis for Highways* (New York: International Textbooks, 1969).

10. American Association of State Highway Officials, Committee on Highway Planning and Design Policies. *Road User Benefits for Highway Improvements* (Washington, D.C., 1960).

11. Stanford Research Institute. *The Value of Time for Passenger Cars* (Menlo Park, Calif. 1967).

12. U.S. Bureau of Public Roads. *Highway Capacity Manual* (Washington, D.C.: U.S. Government Printing Office, 1950).

CHAPTER SIX

1. R.G.D. Allen. *Mathematical Analysis for Economists* (New York: St. Martin's Press, 1971).

2. Charles Ellet, Jr. *An Essay on the Laws of Trade in Reference to the Works of Internal Improvement in the United States* (Richmond, Va.: P.D. Bernard, 1839).

3. Paul J. Garfield and Wallace F. Lovejoy. *Public Utility Economics* (Englewood Cliffs, N.J.: Prentice-Hall, 1964).

4. James M. Henderson and Richard E. Quandt. *Microeconomic Theory.* 2d ed. (New York: McGraw-Hill, 1971).

5. Jack Hirshleifer. "Peak Loads and Efficient Pricing: Comment." *Quarterly Journal of Economics* 72 (1958): 451–462.

6. John R. Meyer et al. *The Economics of Competition in the Transportation Industries* (Cambridge, Mass.: Harvard University Press, 1959).

7. Peter O. Steiner. "Peak Loads and Efficient Pricing." *Quarterly Journal of Economics* 71 (1957): 585–610.

8. _____ . "Peak Loads and Efficient Pricing: Reply." *Quarterly Journal of Economics* 72 (1958): 465–468.

9. The Babcock and Wilcox Company. *Steam: Its Generation and Use.* 37th ed. New York, 1955.

10. U.S. Bureau of Public Roads. *Final Report of the Highway Cost Allocation Study* (Washington, D.C.: U.S. Government Printing Office, 1961).

11. _____ . *Supplementary Report on the Highway Cost Allocation Study* (Washington, D.C.: U.S. Government Printing Office, 1965).

CHAPTER SEVEN

1. Martin Beckmann, C.B. McGuire, and Christopher B. Winsten. *Studies in the Economics of Transportation* (New Haven: Yale University Press, 1956), Part II.
2. Gabriel Dessus. "Rate Fixing in Public Utilities." In James R. Nelson, ed. *Marginal Cost Pricing in Practice* (Englewood Cliffs, N.J.: Prentice-Hall, 1964), pp. 42–44.
3. William Feller. *An Introduction to Probability Theory and Its Applications.* Vol. I (New York: John Wiley, 1957).
4. James C. Nelson. *Railroad Transportation and Public Policy.* (Washington, D.C.: The Brookings Institution, 1959).
5. Alan A. Walters. "The Allocation of Joints Costs with Demands as Probability Distributions." *American Economic Review* 50 (June 1960): 419–432.

CHAPTER EIGHT

1. Robin W. Boadway. "The Welfare Foundations of Cost-Benefit Analysis." *Economic Journal* 84 (December 1964): 926–939.
2. John R. Hicks. "Foundations of Welfare Economics." *Economic Journal* 49 (December 1939): 696–712.
3. ———— . *A Revision of Demand Theory* (London: Oxford University Press, 1956).
4. Herbert Mohring. "Alternative Welfare Gain and Loss Measures." *Western Economic Journal* 9 (December 1971): 349–368.
5. Tibor Scitovsky. "A Note on Welfare Propositions in Economics." *Review of Economic Studies* 14 (November 1941): 77–81.

CHAPTER NINE

1. H.C. Bos and L.M. Koyck. "The Appraisal of Road Construction Projects: A Practical Example." *The Review of Economics and Statistics* 43 (February 1961): 13–20.
2. Robert T. Brown and Clell G. Harral. "Estimating Highway Benefits in Underdeveloped Countries." *Highway Research Record* 115, (1965): 29–43.
3. Ann Fetter Friedlaender. *The Interstate Highway System: A Study in Public Investment* (Amsterdam: North-Holland Press, 1965).
4. Paul A. Samuelson. *Economics.* 8th ed. (New York: McGraw-Hill, 1970).
5. J. Tinbergen. "The Appraisal of Road Construction: Two Calculation Schemes." *The Review of Economics and Statistics* 39 (August 1957): 241–249.

CHAPTER TEN

1. Charles Ellet. *An Essay on the Laws of Trade.* . .(Richmond, Va.: P.D. Bernard, 1839).
2. Herbert Mohring. "Land Values and the Measurement of Highway Benefits." *Journal of Political Economy* 69 (June 1961): 236–249.
3. Johann H. vonThunen. *Der Isolierte Staat.* . .(Hamburg, 1826).
4. Alan A. Walters. *The Economics of Road User Charges* (Washington, D.C.: International Bank for Reconstruction and Development, 1968).
5. U.S. Bureau of Public Roads. *Final Report of the Highway Cost Allocation Study.* Part VI, *Studies of the Economic and Social Impact of Highway Improvement* (Washington, D.C.: U.S. Government Printing Office, 1961).

CHAPTER ELEVEN

1. John Hicks. *A Revision of Demand Theory* (London: Oxford University Press, 1954).
2. Herbert Mohring and Mitchell Harwitz. *Highway Benefits: An Analytical Framework* (Evanston, Ill.: Northwestern University Press, 1962).
3. Herbert Mohring and Harold F. Williamson, Jr. "Scale and 'Industrial Reorganization' Economies of Transport Improvements." *Journal of Transport Economics and Policy* 3 (September 1969): 251–271.
4. Adam Smith. *The Wealth of Nations.* 5th ed. (New York: Modern Library, 1937).
5. U.S. Bureau of Public Roads. *Final Report of the Highway Cost Allocation Study.* Part VI, *Studies of the Economic and Social Impact of Highway Improvements.* (Washington, D.C.: U.S. Government Printing Office, 1961).

CHAPTER TWELVE

1. Leslie Cookenboo, Jr. "Costs of Operating Crude Oil Pipelines." *The Rice Institute Pamphlet: Studies in Economics* (Houston, Tex. 1954).
2. George W. Douglas and James C. Miller III. *Economic Regulation of Domestic Air Transport: Theory and Policy* (Washington, D.C., The Brookings Institution, 1974).
3. Theodore E. Keeler et al. *Optimal Peakload Pricing, Investment, and Service Levels on Urban Expressways.* Working Paper No. 253, Institute of Urban and Regional Development (Berkeley, Calif.: University of California, April 1975).
4. John R. Meyer, John F. Kain, and Martin Wohl. *The Urban Transportation Problem* (Cambridge, Mass.: Harvard University Press, 1965).

5. Herbert Mohring. "Urban Highway Investments." In Robert Dorfman, ed. *Measuring Benefits of Government Investments* (Washington, D.C.: The Brookings Institution, 1965), pp. 331–374.

6. ———. "Optimization and Scale Economies in Urban Bus Transportation." *American Economic Review* 62 (September 1972): 591–604.

7. Alan A. Walters. *The Economics of Road User Charges.* World Bank Staff Occasional Papers (Baltimore, Md.: Johns Hopkins Press, 1968).

8. U.S. Bureau of Public Roads. *Highway Capacity Manual* (Washington, D.C.: U.S. Government Printing Office, 1950).

9. U.S. Civil Aeronautics Board. *Aircraft Operating Cost and Performance Report* (Washington, D.C.: U.S. Government Printing Office, 1973).

Index

Aircraft operating costs, 138-140, 159-163

Airline scheduling, 80-83, 157-163

Allen, R.G.D., 69*n*

American Association of Highway Officials, 16, 18, 25, 45

Average variable costs, defined, 5-6 (*see also* Cost schedules; Marginal cost prices)

Babcock and Wilcox Co., 67

Back-haul pricing, 61-62

Baumol, William, 12*n*

Beckmann, Martin, 76-80

Bessley, M.E., 48-51, 54-57

Benefits (*see* Consumer's surplus benefits; External benefits; Project net benefits; Real income change benefits)

Bergsonian social welfare function (*see* Social welfare function)

Boadway, Robin W., 90*n*

Bos, H.C., 2*n*, 106

Brown, Robert T., 2*n*, 106

Bus (*see* Mass transit)

Classification in rail yards, 77-79

Coleman, R.R., 16-17, 29

Compensation principle, 90, 92
  relation to cost-benefit criterion, 90*n*
  and social welfare function, 90-91

Competition, defined, 8

Competitive equilibrium (*see* Equilibrium, conditions for)

Congestion:
  and auto travel time, 16-19, 29-34
  defined, 15-16
  and fuel consumption, 16
  in railroad activities, 76-77, 79-80

Constant returns to scale:
  defined, 9*n*, 69*n*
  meaning in road construction, 20*n*

Consumer's surplus benefits, 85, 87-89, 92-96, 109-113
  aggregation of, 89-91
  relation to: industrial reorganization, 130-134
    national income change, 2, 110-113
    project net benefits, 92-94, 98-104, 119-125
    real income change, 89, 132, 133*n*

Cookenboo, Leslie, Jr., 137-138

Cope, B.M., 57

Cost allocation, 1-2, 59-74
  with fixed output proportions, 60-62
  main-haul v. back-haul, 61-62
  peak load, 59-60, 62-67
  public utility, 1-2, 59-60, 66-67
  road, 1-2, 60, 70-74
  standards for, in Highway Revenue Act of 1956, 70-74

Cost schedules:
  fixed proportions or type II, 6-7, 63-66, 75-76, 79
  shape of railroad's, 76-80
  variable proportions or type I, 6-8, 63-64, 66-67, 79-80

Cost variations:
  alternative, with output, 6-8
  with random demand, 80-83

Costs (*see* Aircraft operating costs; Constant returns to scale; Cost allocation; Cost schedules; Marginal cost prices; Mass transit, operating costs; Opportunity cost; Road capacity, cost of; Scale economies)

Cost-benefit criterion, 90*n*

Dead-weight loss from non-marginal cost prices, 99–104
Decentralization of competitive equilibrium, 12
Dessus, Gabriel, 81*n*
Differences between transportation and other activities, 1–3
Diminishing returns, law of (*see* Law of diminishing returns)
Diseconomies of scale in road networks, 144–145
Douglas, George, W., 159*n*, 161–163

Eastern Airlines shuttle service, 81–83, 157–158
Economies of scale (*see* Scale economies)
Efficiency:
    of competitive equilibrium, 13
    defined, 13
    and laissez-faire, 13–14
    (*see also* Equilibrium, conditions for)
Efficient transportation prices (*see* Marginal cost prices)
Electricity capacity optimization, 66–67
Ellet, Charles, Jr., 62*n*, 115*n*
Equilibrium, conditions for:
    in competitive industry, 8–12, 61–65, 70
    with fixed input coefficient processes, 11–12, 63–67, 75–76
    with fixed output proportions, 61–62
    in land markets, 46–47
    in transportation activities, 18–24, 65–66, 70–74
    with variable output proportions, 67–70
Euler's theorem, 67–70
Expected cost and output with random demand, 81–83, 157–158
Expressway (*see* Road)
External benefits, 2–3, 12, 85–86, 91–92, 106
    cancellation of, with marginal cost prices, 91–97
    industrial reorganization, 127–134
    land value increases, 115–125
Externality, technological, defined, 12*n*
    (*see also* External benefits)

Family structure, effect on auto opportunity cost, 55–57
Fares (*see* Marginal cost prices)
Feller, William, 82*n*
Ferguson, C.E., 5*n*
Friedlaender, Ann Fetter, 106

Garfield, Paul J., 1*n*, 59*n*
Gauthier, C.L., 57
Gould, J.P., 5*n*

Gronau, Reuben, 52–55

Harrall, Clell G., 2*n*, 106
Harwitz, Mitchell, 133*n*
Henderson, James M., 59*n*
Hicks, John R., 88*n*, 89*n*, 90*n*, 132
Higgins, Benjamin, 2
Highway (*see* Congestion; Cost allocation; Marginal cost prices; Road capacity; Scale diseconomies in road networks; Scale economies, road construction; Scale economies, road use; Travel time, and road volume-capacity ratio)
Hirshleifer, Jack, 67*n*

Industrial reorganization benefits, 127–134

Kain, John F., 143
Keeler, Theodore E., 142–143
Koyck, L.M., 2*n*, 106

Land values, effect on transportation improvements on, 115–125
Law of diminishing returns:
    defined, 6
    and road travel time, 17
Lisco, Thomas E., 50–52, 54–57
Long run, defined, 5
Long run equilibrium (*see* Equilibrium)
Lovejoy, Wallace F., 1*n*, 59*n*
Lump sum tax, 86

McGuire, C.B., 76–80
Mansfield, Edwin, 5*n*
Marginal cost prices:
    compared for transportation and other commodities, 20–21
    with fixed output proportions, defined, 61
    for highway and city street trips, 18–20, 30–34
    implications for measuring project net benefits, 91–97
    for mass transit trips, 153–157
    as quasi-rents for transportation capacity, 20–21, 65–66, 92–96
    relation to: transportation capacity costs, 20–24, 30–34, 61–62, 64–65, 72–73
        travel time value, 18, 30–34, 37–39
        U.S. highway user charges, 99, 104
    as seen by traveler, 28, 30–31, 37–38, 47–54
Marginal travel time per trip and volume-capacity ratio, 17–18
Maslove, Allan, 47, 55
Mass transit, 33, 80, 145–157

operating costs, 37n, 149-157
profitability, 2-3
scale economies in, 145-157
schedule optimization, 37-39, 80, 145-157
subsidy arguments, 2-3, 26-27, 33-35, 147-148
Meyer, John R., 1n, 60n, 143
Miller, James C., III, 159n, 161-163
Miller, William, 3, 26
Mohring, Herbert, 17n, 33n, 46-47, 87n, 91n, 115n, 128n, 133n, 145, 147n, 151n

National income change benefits, 2, 105-113
    relation to consumer's surplus, 2, 110-113
Nelson, James C., 77n
Net benefits (*see* Project net benefits)
Nonuser benefits (*see* External benefits)

Opportunity cost of auto, effect of family structure on, 55-57
Optimization:
    of bus schedules, 37-39, 80, 145-157
    of electricity capacity, 66-67
    of factory size, effect of transportation costs on, 128-133
    of road capacity, 20-21, 24, 29-33, 37-39, 65-66, 70-74
    of train length, 77-78, 145-147

Pareto optimum (*see* Efficiency; Marginal cost prices)
Peak load pricing, 62-67
Pendleton, William C., 47
Pipeline production function, 137-138
Poisson distribution, 81-82, 151, 158, 160, 161n
Profits, accounting v. economic definitions, 8n
Project net benefits, 91-104, 118-124
    in absence of marginal cost prices, 98-104
    with marginal cost prices, 91-97
    relation to: consumers' surplus benefits, 92-94, 98-104, 119-125
        industrial reorganization, 130-133
        rents and quasi-rents, 92-104, 119-125
Public utilities, 1-2, 65-67

Quandt, Richard E., 59n
Quasi-rents:
    defined, 8-9
    relation to: long run equilibrium capital

cost, 10-11, 21-24, 64-67, 147-148
    project net benefits, 91-92
    (*see also* Rents)

Railroad operations, 76-80, 145-147
Randomness in demand, effect on costs of, 80-83, 157-163
Real income change benefits, 86-87, 92
    relation to consumer's surplus, 89, 132, 133n
Rents, 9n, 116-125
    relation to project net benefits, 119-125
    (*see also* Quasi-rents)
Road (*see* Congestion; Cost allocation, Marginal cost prices; Road capacity; Scale diseconomies in road networks; Scale economies, road construction; Scale economies, road use; Travel time, and road volume-capacity ratio)
Road capacity, 29, 142
    cost of, 29n, 142-145
    optimum level of, in Twin Cities, 33
    principles for optimizing, 20-24, 29-33, 37-39, 65-67, 70-74

Samuelson, Paul A., 91n, 105n
Scale diseconomies in road networks, 144-145
Scale economies, 76n, 135-163
    aircraft operation, 138-140, 159, 161
    airline scheduling, 157-163
    bulk transactions, 135, 137-157
    massed reserves, 136, 157-163
    multiples, 135-136, 158
    pipelines, 137-138
    railroad, 145-147
    road construction, 140-143
    road use, 142
Scitovsky, Tibor, 91n
Short run, defined, 5
Short run equilibrium (*see* Equilibrium, conditions for)
Short run marginal costs, defined, 5-6
    (*see also* Cost schedules; Marginal cost prices)
Short run output variations, sources of, 5
Six-tenths rule, 137-140
Smith, Adam, 127
Social overhead capital, 2-3
Social welfare function, 38-39, 89-90
    implications of compensation principle for, 90-91
Square root principle, 80, 145-146, 150, 152-155
Stanford Research Institute, 43n
Steiner, Peter O., 67n
Street (*see* Congestion; Cost allocation;

Marginal cost prices; Road capacity;
Scale diseconomies in road networks;
Scale economies, road construction;
Scale economies, road use; Travel
time, and road volume-capacity ratio)
Strotz, Robert, 37*n*
Subsidies, 2–3, 14, 26–27, 33–35
  magnitude of, for marginal cost prices
    with scale economies, 147–148
  mass transit, 2–3, 26–27, 147–148, 155
  undesirability of, in competitive markets,
    13–14

Technological externality, defined, 12*n*
  (*see also* External benefits)
Tinbergen, Jan, 2*n,* 106
Tolls (*see* Marginal cost prices)
Train length optimization, 77–78, 145–147
Travel price as seen by traveler, 28, 30–31,
  37–38, 47–54
Travel time, and road volume-capacity
  ratio, 16–19, 29–30, 99
Travel time value, 18, 58
  of air and bus travelers, 52–54, 58
  of commuters, 48–52
  differences with travel activity, 49–52,
    55–57

differences among travelers, 26–27, 58
  and capacity optimization, 28–33, 37–
    39
  and mode choice, 30–35, 47–54
  estimation from: location choice, 46–47
  mode and route choice, 47–54
  speed choice, 44–45
  importance in road trip costs, 25–26
  relation to income, 41–42, 48, 50–51,
    53–54, 58
  of shippers, 42–43
Traveler to Callais paradox, 81

U.S. Bureau of Public Roads, 1*n,* 45, 60*n,*
  71*n,* 115*n,* 128*n,* 142–143
U.S. Civil Aeronautics Board, 138, 140

Value of travel time (*see* Travel time value)
Vickrey, William, 145*n*
von Thunen, Johann H., 115*n*

Walters, Alan A., 81, 115*n,* 143
Williamson, Harold F., Jr., 128*n*
Winfrey, Robley, 44–45
Winsten, Christopher B., 76–80
Wohl, Martin, 143

About the Author

Herbert Mohring is professor of economics at the University of Minnesota's Twin Cities campus. With interruptions for visiting professorships at Johns Hopkins, Toronto, and York, he has been a member of the Minnesota faculty since 1961. He is the author of professional journal articles on transportation economics, price theory, and industrial organization and (with Mitchell Harwitz) of *Highway Benefits: An Analytical Framework* (Northwestern University Press: 1962). A graduate of Williams College and Massachusetts Institute of Technology, he is married, has three sons, and lives in Minneapolis.